The Palgrave Lacan Series

Jacques Lacan is one of the most important and influential thinkers of the 20th century. The reach of this influence continues to grow as we settle into the 21st century, the resonance of Lacan's thought arguably only beginning now to be properly felt, both in terms of its application to clinical matters and in its application to a range of human activities and interests. The Palgrave Lacan Series is a book series for the best new writing in the Lacanian field, giving voice to the leading writers of a new generation of Lacanian thought. The series will comprise original monographs and thematic, multi-authored collections. The books in the series will explore aspects of Lacan's theory from new perspectives and with original insights. There will be books focused on particular areas of or issues in clinical work. There will be books focused on applying Lacanian theory to areas and issues beyond the clinic, to matters of society, politics, the arts and culture. Each book, whatever its particular concern, will work to expand our understanding of Lacan's theory and its value in the 21st century.

More information about this series at
http://www.palgrave.com/gp/series/15116

Ed Pluth · Cindy Zeiher

On Silence

Holding the Voice Hostage

palgrave
macmillan

Ed Pluth
California State University, Chico
Chico, CA, USA

Cindy Zeiher
University of Canterbury
Christchurch, Canterbury
New Zealand

The Palgrave Lacan Series
ISBN 978-3-030-28146-5 ISBN 978-3-030-28147-2 (eBook)
https://doi.org/10.1007/978-3-030-28147-2

Cover illustration: Tetra Images—David Engelhardt/Gettyimages

This Palgrave Pivot imprint is published by the registered company Springer Nature Switzerland AG
The registered company address is: Gewerbestrasse 11, 6330 Cham, Switzerland

Acknowledgements

It would be rather remiss to remain silent regarding those who have helped us along the way. We are eternally grateful to our editor, Joanna O'Neill who has shown infinite patience and support throughout the writing of this book. We would like to acknowledge the series editors, Calum Neill and Derek Hook for their enthusiasm of this project.

There are our friends and colleagues who have shown support through their conversations and engagement with the tricky subject of silence: Jelica Šumič-Riha, Russell Sbriglia, Molly Rothenberg, Mladen Dolar, Nick Derrick.

Finally, there are those in our lives who realise that the only way to support us co-authoring a book is to simply remain silent and let us get on with it. Here we thank our silent partners, An Bulkens and Reuben Derrick. And we are also thankful to those who in our deliberations of silence, absolutely refuse this command: our children, Oscar Pluth, Naima and Iris Derrick.

Praise for *On Silence*

"Nothing is easier than to spit out some profound insight about silence as the expression of deep wisdom; it is much more difficult to systematically analyse the multiple ways silence can function: silence as a simple sign of ignorance, silence as a sign that one is overwhelmed by too much to say (or by something that is too traumatic to be put into words)... There are silences and silences: when one talks all the time just so that the thing that really matters is not mentioned, this is also a mode of practicing silence, and when one keeps silent instead of providing the expected reply, this silence can be more revealing than all the words. Pluth and Zeiher's *On Silence* provides a systematic exposition of the different modalities of silence, demonstrating that silence, not external reality, is the real object around which words circulate. The book combines the highest conceptual stringency with a clear and witty style which makes it insanely readable. If *On Silence* will not become an instant classic, then it is better for us, philosophers and other thinkers, to just shut up."

—Slavoj Žižek, *European Graduate School, Switzerland, University of Ljubljana, Slovenia, New York University, USA and Birkbeck Institute for the Humanities, UK*

"This compact, lively book makes an invaluable case for silence as an essential concept linking philosophy and psychoanalysis. From their critical examination of the ethical implications of apophasis to their exploration of the pragmatics of silence in psychoanalytic treatment, Pluth and Zeiher nimbly extricate us from clichés about silence as the beyond of language. Drawing on an astonishing range of references, the authors deliver surprise after surprise: those familiar with Lacanian psychoanalysis will find fresh insights into the intertwined logics of silence and signifier relevant to analytic theory and practice, while those interested in the history of the concept of silence will be rewarded with original readings of philosophers of being and language from the Greeks to the present day. Without sacrificing an iota of rigor, the authors write in a clear and humorous way, leading the reader on an enjoyable journey through complex arguments that will be engaging for undergraduates as well as revelatory to specialists. It is essential reading."

—Molly Anne Rothenberg, *Professor of English, Tulane University, USA*

"'The rest is silence', says Hamlet, and dies, leaving us with an enigmatic and cumbersome rest at the dawn of modernity, a rest which is not even a something. 'The eternal silence of these infinite spaces frightens me,' said Pascal a good half-century later, further imposing on us this unfathomable object that modernity will have to deal with. Ed Pluth and Cindy Zeiher take us on a stunning tour that explores all the facets of this elusive object, tackling the essential relation between silence and language, the inherent negativity and apophasis, the fullness and the void, offering us new readings of the philosophical tradition as well as of Beckett, Melville, Claudel, Cage … All this with a firm red thread in their hands, that of the psychoanalytic take on silence as the essential guideline of its theory and practice, and of Lacan's intervention that doesn't cease to surprise and inspire."

—Professor Mladen Dolar, *University of Ljubljana, Slovenia; Author of* A Voice and Nothing More

Contents

List of Figures

CHAPTER 1

Silence, the Impossible Object

If only what we cannot speak about consented to be silent.
J.-C. Milner (1995, p. 169)

Abstract In this chapter, we contrast a Lacanian approach to silence and language with another historically significant approach to the topics, studied and presented in detail by William Franke in a series of books, which we call apophatic discourse. We determine that the silence portrayed in this discourse is an imaginarized, impossible object, and we discuss how it manifests in some clinical cases Lacan discussed (Dora and the Papin sisters) as well as in his formulas for sexuation.

Keywords Lacan · Hegel · Kojève · Silence · Language · Negation · Apophatic discourse · Franke (William) · The Papin sisters

Who doesn't crave a bit of silence now and then? But what are we looking for from it? Why do we sometimes seem to expect more from it than a brief pause, or mere rest and relaxation: why do we sometimes expect from it something more deeply restorative—presumably the goal of a silent retreat? And why is it that we continue to yearn for silence even after we know quite well that we can never get it completely? The infamous Zen koan—"what is the sound of one hand clapping?"—expresses something of the near mystical fascination we have with silence. We seem to imagine that if it could be obtained egotism, rationality, the

E. Pluth and C. Zeiher, *On Silence*, The Palgrave Lacan Series,
https://doi.org/10.1007/978-3-030-28147-2_1

self…all might be overcome. Silence promises a restoration of subjective wholeness and a way to forget lack. Yet doesn't this make our desire for silence into something nihilistic? Why not just render ourselves comatose instead?

Since we are taking a Lacanian approach to silence here, we are going to do the entirely expected thing and consider silence in terms of the three registers of the imaginary, symbolic, and real. But we promise that in doing so there will be a few surprises! We're not going to go so far as to say that we have discovered, through our reflections on silence, a fourth dimension (as nice as that would be…). We do think we can show, however, that a Lacanian framework can shed light on the different appeals silence has for us, on the different relationships to (and expectations toward) silence that we have. We also think that a new perspective on Lacanian theory and practice is opened up by reflecting on silence. For a thinker who defines us as speaking beings, and who famously claims that even our unconscious is structured like a language, Lacan turns out to be someone who gives silence a very distinct and important function. As we will discuss in our Chapter 2, Lacanian psychoanalysis can even be considered, as Mladen Dolar put it, a pragmatics of silence (2006).

But let's start with a bit of orientation. We can create a (somewhat precarious, perhaps overly positivist and even misleading) structuralist presentation of our trajectory. We start with an opposed pair, language and silence, and a possible over-valuation (represented by a plus sign) or under-valuation (represented by a minus sign) of each. In this scenario there would then be four possible positions on language and silence, which we can associate with a variety of disciplines, worldviews, discourses:

Language	Silence	
+	+	Lacanian psychoanalysis
+	-	empty speech, logorrhea, the anxiety of silence
-	+	apophatic discourse, mysticism, logophobia
-	-	the tragic worldview, depression, melancholia

First, we want to point out that we do think it should be possible to value both language and silence equally highly. This is how we will portray the rather unique position that Lacanian psychoanalysis adopts. If silence and language are held in equally high esteem, silence is not taken to be something that compensates for the malaise of language, nor is language something one clings to as a defence against whatever might be threatening about silence. (We will be saying much more about both of these views later.) Getting ahead of ourselves a bit, in theoretical terms we can say that in this position it is possible for the speaking subject to be invested in its own division, rather than trying to avoid it or overcome it (although arguably we are invested in both). This double valuation of language and silence is in fact part of the reason why we want to say that any seeming opposition between language and silence is actually overcome in Lacanian theory and practice—hence, our structuralist matrix is misleading (so we have already started with a negation of our own proposition, which is typical of how we think silence operates). The topological relationship between language and silence in Lacanian theory and practice is quite different from how the relationship shakes out in the other positions, in which silence is generally taken as a beyond, something on the other side of language as it were, either positively or negatively charged.

But let us continue with describing the positions on our matrix: in a second position, language is over-valued and silence acquires a negative connotation. This position can be found in forms of excessive chatter (*logorrhea*). The first-generation psychoanalyst Karl Abraham identified this trait in 1927 and linked it to the oral stage in his essay *The Influence of Oral Eroticism on Character Formation*:

> With these subjects, we encounter certain character traits that oblige us to refer to a curious displacement to the interior of the oral domain. Their ardent desire for satisfaction by sucking is transformed into a need to *give* by the mouth, so much so that we discover in them, beyond a permanent desire to obtain everything, a constant need to communicate orally with others. Logorrhea is the result, connected in most cases to a feeling of plenitude. These subjects have the impression that the wealth of their thought is inexhaustible, and they attribute to their words a special power or an exceptional value. (Abraham, in Nasio [1987, p. 72])

We all know people who love to incessantly chatter about what they supposedly know! (And some of us, frankly, are people like this…) Abraham does not mention the status of silence in logorrhea, but Lacan does when he observes that an obsessive's logorrhea is an attempt to fill in the gaps in the Other's discourse—the silences between signifiers that are associated with the troubling presence of the Other's desire. This is way of understanding both how a logorrheic analysand may deal with silence in the analytic session and how obsessional neurosis generally tends to reduce desire into demand: replacing or reducing the obscurity of the Other's desire, expressed just as well in silences as in signifiers, to the more familiar, recognizable signifiers of demand (a topic we will explore in Chapter 2).

Much more common, and much more culturally significant, we think, is the third position, in which language is devalued and silence promoted. We'll get back to this in a moment.

Jumping ahead to the fourth position, in which a pox is put on both language and silence, we first want to ask: is this actually a viable position? We think that to maintain it would require a truly tragic worldview, bemoaning the vanity of both silence and language. Maybe only Pascal, the first modern "tragic individual" (if Lucien Goldmann's 1964 analysis in his *The Hidden God* is correct) can be situated here. We'll explore Goldmann's reading of Pascal in our final chapter. We think that if his account is right, Pascal's position can be portrayed as a transitional, dialectical moment on the way to creating the conditions for the possibility of the psychoanalytic-Lacanian perspective. Perhaps it is Pascal and not Descartes who presents us with the first modern subject. We think that a shift in the very status of silence itself is key to this point, and we think this is what Lacan chronicles in some ways when he discusses the emergence of psychoanalysis in the wake of the *cogito* and the modern sciences, and in his own discussions of Pascal.

We want to spend the rest of this chapter on the philosophical assumptions behind the third position, in which silence is highly valued at the cost of a devaluation of language itself. This is a view with lasting social and psychological appeal: it is bound up with what we were describing in our opening paragraph.

Something that we think is interesting about Alain Badiou's philosophy will take us to where we want to go. What is typically thought to make Alain Badiou unique among recent philosophers is his claim that the task of doing ontology—the very task Heidegger made into philosophy's privilege—should be handed over to a branch of mathematics (specifically, set theory). Badiou's interest in mathematics alone is enough to place him at odds with a dominant tendency in philosophy, one that he calls into question and that he refers to as the linguistic turn. While the linguistic turn commonly refers to the position of early analytic philosophers, in several different places Badiou has made the important observation that both analytic and continental philosophy, despite their sharp differences on nearly everything else, can in fact both be placed under this heading. This insight about a hidden unity between two very different traditions deserves more attention, and will set the scene for our interrogation into how and why language is given a negative evaluation in a tradition we will being paying close attention to in this chapter.

Badiou's view of the linguistic turn can be put this way: it leads directly to anti-philosophy. When philosophy starts asking questions about language itself, its death is imminent. This may be one of the reasons why Badiou himself does not to our knowledge ever make language itself into an explicit topic or theme in his philosophy: what the linguistic turn and anti-philosophy seem to have taught him is that thinking about language is toxic for doing philosophy. Language is philosophy's ultimate impasse: philosophy gets tripped up when it reflects on language. In order to be a philosopher, is it necessary to not problematize language? We inevitably think of Hegel here and indeed any philosopher who is committed to the view that philosophy can and should be practiced in ordinary language as a way to elucidate and elaborate upon an idea.

Of course, this intervention is not about Alain Badiou, the linguistic turn, or even anti-philosophy, although we inevitably touch on these areas throughout. It's about silence. But these questions and deliberations about language and its limits, and the very possibility of thinking, are good places to begin our exploration of the philosophical presuppositions involved in putting silence in very high esteem, while at the same time lowering the value of language itself. We could say that we're engaged here in what looks like a Kantian transcendental endeavour: we are exploring the conditions for the possibility of any valuing or privileging of silence over language—an exploration we admit is conducted at our own peril, since in writing about silence we're committed to a linguistic treatment of it! And so, we are going to start our discussion with what we would qualify, in Lacanian terms, as a position in which silence is imaginarised.

William Franke calls it the apophatic tradition. According to him, an apophatic discourse is one that "consists of words that negate themselves in order to evoke what is beyond words – and indeed beyond the limits of language altogether" (2007b, pp. 1, 2). *Apophasis* in Greek literally evokes a "saying away" or a moving "away from speech," and it can even serve as a term for negation itself. Franke makes much of Aristotle's view that apophasis was a significant part of rhetoric, such that

> 'Apophasis,' the Greek word for 'negation,' may be viewed as inherent in the phenomenon of discourse per se. In fact, a word *is not* what it names or signifies – indeed, to function significantly as word, it *cannot* simply be what it means – and this tacit negation, accordingly, may be found lurking covertly in every word that is uttered. (ibid., p. 9)

Franke brilliantly isolates here one of the main philosophical assumptions of this tradition: apophasis bases itself on what it takes to be a fundamental property of language, negation. Further, negation takes a rather dim view of this property.

Negation is also very important to Lacan's view of language negation, and in this respect his position is in agreement with one aspect of the apophatic tradition. This is even a point at which the analytic and continental traditions diverge. The continental view tends to embrace a view of language in which it is a negating activity, while the analytic view focuses on language from another perspective. Charles Taylor helps us to see this point in his recent book *The Language Animal* (2016). Taylor argues that there are two main traditions for thinking about language in western philosophy. One stems from Hobbes, Locke, and Condillac, and it emphasizes the designating function of language. It approaches language atomistically, assuming that individual words are learned first, one by one. One should think here of Augustine's famous account of language acquisition, according to which people learn words by observing others pointing at things and making the appropriate sounds: a view that is comically problematic, since it presupposes that the language users already possess the basics of the languages they are supposed to be acquiring—that they already possess what Taylor calls the "background understanding which we need to draw on to speak and understand" (ibid., p. 21). Taylor argues against this model and what he sees as its continued predominance (despite modifications) among post-Fregean analytic philosophers. He wishes to argue for the superiority of the view of language that he identifies in the Romantic tradition—the figures of Hamann, Herder, and Humboldt (significantly and rather perplexingly, the Hegel scholar Taylor leaves Hegel off this list!). Taylor is drawn to how this tradition adopts a holistic view, and how it emphasizes what he calls the creative or figuring dimension of language, its world-creating capacity. Although he does not make this point himself, we think that what Taylor likes about this tradition can in fact be thought of in terms of the concept of negation: this tradition avoids the errors of the atomistic, designative (analytic) view of language by embracing language as a negating activity.

Even classical textbook cases of what is called apophasis in rhetoric demonstrate the centrality of this linguistic quality. "I certainly don't need to point out to you how…" or "Of course it goes without saying that…" are cases in which one nevertheless does say, or mention, or call to a listener's or reader's attention what one says one does not need to say. In rhetoric, these are examples of phrases that create by negating. In cases like this it is as if language is making up for its failure or inability to designate by a proliferation of words. What Franke calls the apophatic tradition simply applies the same lesson on a larger scale.

We get a hint of this in Franke's discussion of Beckett's *Waiting for Godot* (1954 [1982]), where he portrays the relationship posited there between words and things this way:

> It is the nature of words as signs to indicate something absent from themselves, something they are not. Conversely what actually is contradicts words and all that they can say – its being is always more or less than what can be signified. (2014, p. 76)

Authors like Beckett (he also adds Pinter and Sarraute) "often expose the arbitrariness of *what* we have said, whether *this or that* -- it hardly matters" (ibid., p. 77). We are not so sure that this is a correct way to portray Beckett's position on language and silence: we will give our own account in Chapter 3. Beckett's characters do seem to be held hostage by language, and they cannot release themselves from it—but it is noteworthy that they do not even seem to try. (Beckett's characters would seem to have either no need nor any interest in a silent retreat!) For example, at the end of *Waiting for Godot*, the two characters, in an attempt to release themselves from boredom, declare to each other, 'Let's go', despite not planning on going anywhere in particular. The words uttered almost may as well not have been said. This is why we want to say that Beckett's characters (perhaps even Beckett himself) are closer to the position in which they suffer from the hold of language. Is this not the very demand of Lacanian psychoanalysis? To somehow declare this suffering of the symptom and handle its effects? We could even say that Beckett and his characters suffer from something like a Stockholm Syndrome regarding language—which is perhaps an adequate way to describe the Lacanian view as well: that they, like all of us, are held hostage by language, and they put up with it by falling in love with their hostage taker. This in itself is only part of the conundrum however: the true confrontation occurs upon the realization that the hostage taker doesn't love you back.

Apophatic discourse, as described by Franke, appreciates that language and the negative go together. But because of this link, this discourse concludes that language is out of joint with being. For this reason, in order to restore a contact with being, it requires language to use its power of negation on itself. In apophatic discourse, a truly adequate statement would be one that points out its necessary failure to signify what it is trying to signify. Apophatic discourse does not always go so far as to silence itself entirely. Instead it typically engages in discursive practices that minimize language's status and pretences. It is a discourse in which language grapples with itself, and it takes this negative practice as a badge of honour, something that restores the dignity of the true and the real.

Since apophatic discourse and Lacanian psychoanalysis both agree on the links between language and negation, we can explore the connections more closely in order to make the differences appear more starkly. To start to get a sense of where they differ, let's consider a passage from Kojève's *Introduction to the Reading of Hegel* (1947) that Lacan liked to riff on in his early seminars. With his typical flair for the dramatic, Kojève writes:

> In Chapter VII of the *Phenomenology*, Hegel said that all *conceptual* understanding (*Begreifen*) is equivalent to a *murder*. Let us, then, recall what he had in view. As long as the Meaning (or Essence, Concept, Logos, Idea, etc.) is embodied in an empirically existing entity, this Meaning or Essence, as well as this entity, lives. For example, as long as the Meaning (or Essence) "dog" is embodied in a sensible entity, this Meaning (Essence) lives: it is the real dog, the living dog which runs, drinks, and eats. But when the Meaning (Essence) "dog" passes in to the *word* "dog" – that is, becomes [an] abstract Concept which is *different* from the sensible reality

> that it reveals by its Meaning – the Meaning (Essence) *dies*: the word "dog" does not run, drink, and eat; in it the Meaning (Essence) *ceases* to live – that is, it dies. And that is why the conceptual understanding of empirical reality is equivalent to a murder. (1947, p. 140)

A remarkable argument! Whatever its merits, we think that Kojève has identified here one of the important philosophical and ethical drivers of the apophatic tradition, and we would like to highlight a couple of things about it. First, there is a clear connection to nominalism. Consider the famous quote from Goethe's *Faust*: *All theory is grey, but forever green is the tree of life*. Words here are taken to be pale abstractions of real things. This is essentially part of what Kojève is saying when he is describing, for example, *dog* as an abstract concept. But it is not its abstraction alone that pits the apophatic tradition against language. It is something else that Kojève is also touching on. Language is considered here not only as an abstraction but as an abstracting *activity*: Kojève brilliantly calls our attention not only to the status of linguistic terms (abstract, general, universal) but also to *what they do*. As Kojève describes it, they can be considered an unjust violation of the (supposed) tranquillity of the real: "The conceptual understanding of empirical reality is equivalent to a murder" (1947, p. 140).

Lacan evokes Kojève's views on this point in his seminar a few decades later, replacing the dog with an elephant, but emphasizing the same points—negation, language as both a productive and destructive activity, and although he does not mention murder, it is not far off:

> It is owing to the fact that the word *elephant* exists in their language, and hence that the elephant enters into their deliberations, that men have been capable of taking, in relation to elephants, even before touching them, decisions which are more far-reaching for these pachyderms than anything else that has happened to them throughout their history – the crossing of a river or the natural decimation of a forest. With nothing more than the word *elephant* and the way in which men use it, propitious or unpropitious things, auspicious or inauspicious things, in any event catastrophic things have happened to elephants long before anyone raised a bow or a gun to them.
>
> Besides, it is clear, all I need do is talk about it, there is no need for them to be here, for them really to be here, thanks to the word *elephant* and to be more real than the contingent elephant-individuals. (1953–1954 [1991], p. 178)

Lacan has a pithier and more explicitly Kojèvian way of making the same point in the *Purloined Letter* (1966 [2002]): *the word is the death of the thing*. Obviously, Lacan aligns himself very closely to what Kojève is arguing. Language is violent, philosophically murderous, and yet, as is only implied in the quote we gave from Kojève (but, since it is a Hegelian point, it should be obvious), it establishes something "more real" than the concrete individuals. The shared (Hegelian) view of Kojève and Lacan is that the death of the thing performed by the word is actually an elevation of the thing itself. Through the word, the thing attains a symbolic immortality—the thing will never die as long as it has a name bestowed upon it. Lacan even calls this new status for a thing its *heightened* reality.

How this differs from how apophatic discourse views the situation is obvious. The view that language negates things, that it is active with respect to them by somehow cancelling them out, or at a minimum "abstracting" them, establishes a fork in the road. At this fork apophatic discourse takes a path that Kojève and Lacan do not take. Apophatic discourse takes up the cause of the murdered dog; Kojève and Lacan are saying they did the dog a service. Let us be clear however that this is a bit misleading: apophatic discourse does not take seriously the idea that things really die because of being named. Apophatic discourse upholds the resistance of things, their immunity and persistent otherness to language—which we are generally blind due to language holding us hostage. For apophatic discourse, the idea that the word is the death of the thing is vanity, pretention…

There is in fact an interesting equivocation in apophatic discourse: it holds that what language does to things is unjust and objectionable, but at the same time, it holds that language doesn't really do anything to them at all! (An example of Freudian "kettle logic" here.) Advocates of apophasis agree that language is active, and that it negates: what the discourse of apophasis wishes to do, however, is to turn the negation against language itself, probably out of a sense of justice. Language becomes something like a deceptive hostage taker then—it *tricks us* into thinking it has done something to things, but it really hasn't. Or, language is like a kidnapper running a bluff all the while hiding important stuff from us. Apophatic discourse holds that this illusion needs to be corrected, and the way to do so, short of embracing silence altogether (which is of course always a temptation for this discourse, we will show later) is to turn the negating capacity of language against itself. Ironically, language's practice of self-negation is the only way, within language, for linguistic beings to attest to, if not expose, the persistent alterity, brilliance, and resistance of what is beyond language. This forms the basis for a sort of ethical or pragmatic nominalism: a call to circumvent language and restore direct contact with the particulars of the real by using language against itself. One can imagine the endless, deconstructive, Derridean manoeuvres this inspires.

As Franke points out, correctly, Hegel, despite being influenced by aspects of apophatic discourse (especially by thinkers like Cusa, Boehme, and Silesius Angelus), is the antithesis to this discourse because of his view that "everything that is real *can* be said" (2007b, pp. 2, 12). However, we think the distinction between actuality and existence in Hegel's work may be overlooked here. Due to the trivial status Hegel gives to mere existence, it would not matter much whether anything could be said of it at all. Or, whatever there is to say of it is of very little of interest—"*so ist Es*" as Hegel said, evidently underwhelmed at the landscape before him when his friends took him to the Alps. So, in a sense, Hegel might agree with Franke's point: there are some things that resist being said. But their moment of departure lies in that Hegel simply disagrees about their importance: the fact that they cannot be said is connected to the fact that they do not matter. However, Franke is certainly right that when it comes to actuality, where the real and the rational are fused. For from Hegel's perspective there is indeed nothing about this that is ineffable.

Interestingly, Hegel and apophatic discourse, as disparate as they are, have something rather surprising in common: a positive assessment of the ontological argument for God's existence. However, Franke takes Anselm's argument to be establishing God as that which is beyond our capacity to think and verbalize, while Hegel reads it in exactly the opposite way! As Franke's scholarship establishes, some of the most important preconditions for Anselm's argument are to be found in the Neoplatonic tradition, which emphasized the notion of God as a One that is beyond being. But why beyond being? The phrase, of course, is famously used by Socrates in *Book VII* of *The Republic* in reference to the Good. When Socrates's frustrated interlocutors push him on how he understands the Good—is it pleasure? Knowledge? Something else? Socrates, as usual, confesses his ignorance, laments having merely an opinion of what the Good actually is, but agrees nevertheless to give an account of what he thinks the Good is: and here we can see immediately what the difficulties are. The Good is beyond being, but at the same time can be compared to what certain beings do, or to the status that some (familiar) beings have. For example, the Good can be compared to the sun, and it can be said to play a role similar to the one the sun plays in the visible world (as cause of visibility, as well as existence). However, his main point is the ironic result of the endeavour: the comparison to the sun is just a comparison. Since the Good reigns over all beings, it must therefore must be something other than them, higher than them. So, according to this neo-Platonic reading, the attempt to think the Good itself is an exercise in showing us the limits of thinking and language: such attempts defeat themselves, thereby highlighting the failures and inadequacies of language, and thereby demonstrating that the only thing that can fairly or sensibly said about The Good is something that is a paradox, and strictly unthinkable or inconceivable: the claim that the Good is beyond being. The Good requires us to think beyond being—a phrase we can say, glibly, but of course cannot do, and are not really thinking anything by, just as we can certainly utter the words "square circle" but are not conceiving of anything when we do so. A fine example of what apophasis is here: a discourse keen on cancelling itself out and making sure that the negating capacity of language is primarily turned against itself.

Franke's reading of Anselm goes against the grain of most interpretations of the ontological argument, in which the argument is taken to be far more positive than it is negative. Typically, the upshot of the argument, hopefully familiar to first-year philosophy students everywhere, is that we can establish, with certainty, the existence of God. God is that being higher than which, or greater than which, I cannot conceive of anything else. If God didn't exist, however, then I could conceive of something higher than God…a God (or some other big Other) that would exist. So, I contradict myself if I think God does not exist, and by thinking God does not exist I confess thereby my ignorance of what God is. Therefore, I discover that existence necessarily belongs to God—existence cannot be denied of God without overt contradiction and nonsense: denying God's existence is like denying that a triangle has three sides. And this is why Anselm tells us that only a fool can say God does not exist: such a person does not really know what she is saying. Such a person may as well simply shut-up.

Hegel, in his defence of the ontological argument, focuses on an entirely different aspect of it. For him, it's precisely the argument's effort to grasp the totality that matters. The ontological argument is targeting the right thing, it is orienting thought in the right direction, as far as Hegel is concerned: it is trying to think the whole (and of course, for Hegel, the true is the whole). He takes the argument to be essentially affirming, although rather clumsily, our capacity to know. As Franke pointed out, Hegel holds that everything real can be said: and what is more real than God? As Hegel himself was fond of repeating, God would not a bunch of idiots for his followers: he would want them to know him. (And, to flirt with heresy, one might add that God could not even truly know himself without this knowledge others have of him.) Apophatic discourse holds roughly the opposite: what is most real cannot be said, and the ontological argument actually shows us the unthinkability of God's being. Not being able to be said is, in fact, the very mark of a thing's higher reality. On this view, Christianity becomes the opposite of what Hegel called it—for Hegel, it was the revealed religion. God was no longer obscure or shrouded in mystery, but rather the opposite: by becoming Flesh, he became as knowable as we are to ourselves. For apophatic discourse, if there is any revelation to be had it is not discursive or cognitive—or rather, it happens only in an erasure of discourse in which the *beyond* is revealed negatively.

Franke finds precisely such an erasure in Anselm's argument when he takes it to demonstrate the "intrinsic openness of thinking, including thought's very thinking of its own limits" (2007a, p. 29). Drawing from Karl Barth's interpretation of Anselm evidently, Franke concludes that what makes the ontological argument valid is not a deduction from a conceptual definition, but something more along the lines of a *showing* through the fact of language's failure:

> It is not the concept of God as 'that than which none greater can be thought' [...] but rather the openness of thought to the infinity that is realized in actually thinking this, and so negating every determinate thought as still allowing for something more unlimited and therefore greater, that gives validity to the ontological argument as an actual manifestation of God's infinite being. There is here no logical deduction of God's existence form a necessary concept but, simply, the realization of infinite openness of mind, which is itself the very being of God conceived of as infinite Intellect. This, at any rate, is as much of God in his own essence as can be humanly experienced under the aspect of knowing or intellect. (ibid., p. 29)

Here again we see how Franke's apophatic reading of the ontological argument goes against the grain of most readings of it. Some of what he says places him close to what Hegel sees in the ontological argument, but there are at least two important differences. First, Franke takes the argument to be one that is designed to bring about an *experience* of God through the destruction of language and conceptuality, whereas this is certainly not how Hegel understands it. (This would be like what Hegel alludes to in the Preface to the *Phenomenology of Spirit*: the romantic desire to have the absolute directly, all at once, as if it could be shot out of a cannon.) The second difference we think can be found in Franke's reference to infinity. No doubt Hegel would see here a 'bad infinity' at work—infinity as a merely inaccessible, endless series: an ultimate beyond. This is clear from the fact that Franke portrays the experience of God here as the revelation of a limit and a beyond at the same time. It is the inaccessibility and otherness of God, just as much as it is God's presence, that is revealed to us in the ontological argument according to Franke. This is exactly what Hegel reproaches Kant for in the latter's critique of the ontological argument. For Hegel, it is in (positive) infinity that being and thought are united.

What we have been trying to establish is what we think is a key philosophical assumption of apophatic discourse, brought out very well by Franke's remarkable scholarship and intellectual rigor. Apophatic discourse does not necessarily lead to a preference for silence, or to the sort of ethic of silence we will discuss in a moment. It is one thing to engage in the mental exercises of apophatic discourse, which do seem to have some demonstrative and probably even ethical value; it is another thing to dismiss the value of such linguistic and cognitive endeavours altogether and just be silent. In other words, where for apophatic discourse there is still a sort of pedagogical value in experiencing (and practicing) language's failures, in a full-on ethic of silence such language games can be avoided altogether. Indeed, the title of one of Franke's books is *A Philosophy of the Unsayable*: notably, not a philosophy *of silence*. However, perhaps this should in fact be the title of his book (or, at least, of its sequel); the position of language, the use of language, we think ultimately becomes untenable and indefensible in apophatic discourse, and should lead to the inevitable conclusion that words and discourse are entirely in vain.

Apophatic discourse has everything to do with the relationship between thinking and its outside, with the noise of thought vainly trying to breach the silence of the beyond while always failing to get there. So, it is when language fails, and further, points out its own failures, that it is able to mark the place of the beyond of itself. While Franke signals that silence itself gives the subject some (semblance of a) sovereign moment within language (a way to break through to the other side, as it were), we think that Lacan considers silence instead to be a rather ordinary, even benign, part of language—a silence in and of the symbolic, as we'll explain in our next chapter.

How do we get from apophatic discourse to what Ludwig Wittgenstein (1922 [1981]) articulated best: "whereof one cannot speak, thereof one must remain silent?" Wittgenstein is, we want to say, the most rigorous thinker of apophatic discourse, its culmination point, its logical end point. With his insight, the discursive games valued by apophasis no longer hold any value.

This leads us to consider a certain practice or ethic of silence that was written about quite extensively throughout the Christian tradition. The literature on the virtues of silence in Christianity is too vast to consider here. Let us however present just two samples that bring out the essentials. The first, from the seventh century, by Isaac of Nineveh:

> Silence is the mystery of the world to come. Speech is the organ of this present world. More than all, things love silence: it brings you a fruit that the tongue cannot describe. In the beginning, we have to force ourselves to be silent. But then from our very silence is born something that draws us into deeper silence. May God give you an experience of this 'something' that is born of silence. If you practice this, inexpressible light will dawn upon you. [*A Day in the Life of a Trappist Monk*]

In contrast to apophatic discourse, here it is silence itself—not a discourse incessantly putting itself under erasure—that is taken to be the true pathway to the deity, the way to grace or enlightenment. And we see clearly in this passage an overtly negative evaluation of language as such—"speech is the organ of this present world" (not a good thing for a Christian). What Isaac of Nineveh is saying here is very close to what one can still read today in any number of pitches for long periods of silence: the benefits of silent retreats are supposed to be clarity, better insight into the self, restoration, oneness, authenticity…

Another example from roughly a thousand years later makes this point even more explicit. Abbé Dinouart's *L'art de se taire* (1771), adds a modern, post-Cartesian dimension to the value of silence. It promotes silence not only because it brings the practitioner closer to God, and transports her away from this world, but also explicitly for its ability to make the self whole, to re-establish what Derrida might have called self-presence. Dinouart starts his book by maligning the "new philosophy" of his time as one that promotes nothing but idle chatter, by means of which one can become everything "except…Christian and subject" (ibid., p. 26). Dinouart concedes that there is not only a time when it is appropriate to speak, but that more importantly there is a time when it is appropriate to be silent. And this time should in fact be our default mode: "The time for being quiet should be first in order" (ibid., p. 35). This is in large part because (and here we see room for a Derridean critique of self-presence) he feels that "man never possesses himself more than in silence: beyond that, he seems to spread himself out, so to speak, beyond himself, and to vanish (*se dissiper*) by discourse, such that he is less to or for himself, than to or for others" (p. 35). Dinouart is very clear here about what both silence and language do. Silence restores the self, while language fragments it. While it does not seem like Dinouart engages in apophatic discourse (there seems to be little in his writing about the relationship between God and language, or about the connections between language and negation) his point about the dissipating effects that speaking has on the self resonate with apophatic discourse's suspicions about language and its effects. This is a position that still has quite a bit of appeal, obviously. Even today some of us find ourselves seeking out silent retreats as a way of trying to manage and mediate the effects of being subjects of signifiers.

We turn now to a more explicit Lacanian approach to apophatic discourse. From a Lacanian perspective, the status of silence in apophatic discourse seems to be that of *i(a)*. This may not seem to make much sense: isn't *i(a)* the specular image, my double in the mirror, or that of a rival? But what we have in mind is an elaboration on *i(a)* in relation to *object a*, in which *i(a)* is something like the glamourous covering that the void of *object a* receives: *object a*, non-specularizable as Lacan likes to tell us, is rendered visible in/by *i(a)*. Thus, *i(a)* should be read in Lacanian algebra as the image of the other-object. But here is why we want to connect *i(a)* with the status of silence in apophatic discourse: *i(a)* is something like the empirical object we *think* we desire, behind which lurks something else that we do not know we desire (that is, *object a* proper, which is causing our desire). This also makes *i(a)* into a frustrating object, whose possession and attainment never gives the satisfaction expected.

If *object a* is the cause of desire, and a cause of the subject's division, *i(a)* is the object we hope will heal us. Object a entails castration and loss; *i(a)* promises their overcoming. How silence can take on the status of such an object is put very well by Dolar in his book on the voice:

> Silence can indicate the highest wisdom, and its extension can be a 'mystic silence,' a silence of the universe which can overwhelm and enthral the observer, a vision of supreme harmony, the oceanic feeling that Freud talks about in *Civilization and Its Discontents*, cosmic peace. There are no voices to be heard, and for that very reason the silence speaks in an unalloyed presence, for voices would spoil the equilibrium, the alternation would bring imbalance. Silence functions as saturated with the highest sense, the mirror which reflects the inner and the outer in a perfect match. It is the silence not of a lack but of a supposed plenitude. (2006, p. 155)

Silence in apophatic discourse has a status that we could call that of a full silence (echoing what Lacan called full speech). And we can go back to some of our earlier points here: language marks, divides, splits, and cuts. In extremis, it murders the thing. As Dolar puts it, a voice interrupting silence would bring a certain imbalance between them (2006).

What is the position of the subject in apophatic discourse? Lacan makes a pertinent observation about the subject position adopted in apophatic discourse when he describes the impasse of neurotic desire as an attempt to efface the negative, mortifying effects of the signifier's relationship to things, particularly to the object of desire. This perspective is perhaps first developed in his discussion of courtly love poetry in his seventh seminar. What Lacan is struck by in this tradition is its capacity to elevate a woman to the status of what he calls "the Thing"—a satisfying yet lost object (1959, p. 112). And this happens, necessarily, and only, by converting the desired woman into a signifier—the notorious "Dame" or "Lady," who, Lacan always likes to point out, in all courtly love poetry seems to be essentially the same person, with the same qualities, chief among them being her inaccessibility. More than this is the inscription of the word which gives rise to its very concept. Here he mentions François duc de La Rochefoucauld's 136th maxim: "Some people would never have fallen in love if they had never heard of love" (1962–1963 [2014], p. 209; La Rochefoucauld 1959, p. 54).

When briefly touching on the topic of courtly love two years later in his ninth seminar, Lacan considers how sublimation contains a contradiction: the drive's aim (satisfaction) subsists and is realized in every sublimation, even though sublimation is also a diversion from the drive's (original) aim. What Lacan finds odd about this is that it means that in sublimation there is after all really no repression, no effacement of enjoyment at all. Enjoyment is just re-routed: with sublimation "it is by ways that are apparently contrary to jouissance that jouissance is obtained" (1961–1962 [2002], p. 154). As an example, Lacan considers the status Beatrice had for Dante. Imagine, he says, that Dante did manage at some point to actually fuck Beatrice—and who knows, Lacan adds, maybe he did? Still, this would involve something quite distinct from what he in fact managed to accomplish: turning the person Beatrice into the signifier 'Beatrice'—into a poetic object, we could say. After this, whether intercourse happens or not, there's another satisfaction involved no matter what happens. And anyway, best of luck with trying to fuck a signifier! Clearly, actually sleeping with Beatrice still does not manage accomplish *that*. Yet Lacan's view is that such an impossible fuck is in a sense exactly what the courtly love poet manages to accomplish through the detours of sublimation. Courtly love, as sublimation, turns the sublime Thing into a signifier. And, it is important to add, it sticks with it, tarries with it, and enjoys it by channelling *jouissance* into language use. This seems to be what Lacan admires about courtly love poetry. And here we can see how the idea that the word is the death of the thing takes on another signification, one in which the death of the thing is affirmed and celebrated because it is able to bring about new conditions for enjoyment.

This is quite different from what apophatic discourse is doing. What Lacan says next is, we think, quite important and relevant to our discussion of silence, and it is our first hint of what Lacan's views are on the importance of a shift in the status of both language and silence, one that he for a time associates with the rise of modern science, the Galileo-event. Lacan describes this shift in terms of something that happens to neurotic desire—and, we wish to add, to a point of view that is implied by the subject position in apophatic discourse. Already in his seventh seminar, Lacan had observed that the psychic structure or libidinal economy that fueled courtly love poetry seems to have gone extinct. And nothing has taken its place. What there is instead, Lacan suggests in his ninth seminar, is a new subject position associated with neurotic desire. This is the subject position we want to associate with apophatic discourse.

Lacan is talking about this when he characterizes the contemporary neurotic as an "innocent," a sort of naïve fool who is, however, possessed of a desire to know, a desire to correct her ignorance.[1] In particular, this contemporary subject wants to know what there is of the real, or what is left of the real and what can be accessed of it after language has done its negative work. This already contrasts very sharply with the courtly love poet's ability to get off with a signifier: we take this to mean that the contemporary neurotic is libidinally invested in language to a much lesser degree than courtly love poets were...and, we think that at least in part psychoanalysis takes on the task of re-investing in it. "The neurotic," Lacan tells us, "wants to retransform the signifier into that of which it is the sign" (1961–1962 [2002], p. 155).

We can speak of this neurotic desire in the terms Badiou used to characterize artistic and political movements in the twentieth century: it is a passion for the real. The neurotic wants to believe that there is something of it still there and that if only language would get out of the way it could be attained. This is where the idea of the word being the death of the thing is important yet again, and Lacan's observation now is that the neurotic has repressed this fact. Again, the courtly love poet, by contrast (a good, surprising Hegelian *avant la lettre*?) was able to elevate or revere the signifier over the object. Isn't Lacan positioning himself as a reconstructed courtly love poet when he made the following famous remark in his eleventh seminar?

> Sublimation is nonetheless satisfaction of the drive, without repression.
>
> In other words – for the moment, I am not fucking, I am talking to you. Well! I can have exactly the same satisfaction as if I were fucking. That's what it means. Indeed, it raises the question of whether in fact I am not fucking at this moment. (XI, pp. 165–166)

Neurotic desire errs in thinking that fucking the real Beatrice, not her signifier, would be the key to enjoyment. In fact, what the neurotic is doing is something rather worse than what signifiers do; signifiers may murder the thing. Neurotic desire turns the real Beatrice into $i(a)$.

Notice how Lacan's Hegelianism is unrelenting: the work signifiers do on things is irreversible. The signifier effaces the thing, it wipes

[1] Arguably, perhaps the desire for the contemporary neurotic is to enjoy one's ignorance, which precisely and deliberately locates silence as an effacing signifier.

it out. Lacking the capacity (for whatever reason) to embrace the signifier as such, to get off with it, as courtly love poetry was able to do, neurotic desire amounts to wanting to "efface this effacement"—this is what we call the contemporary neurotic's passion for the real, seeking a restoration of what is lost. This becomes both tragic and comic, since the neurotic's effort to abolish the effacement ironically reinforces it—in the same way that apophatic discourse asserts that it is in contact with the beyond by dwelling on language's failures, while the beyond simply continues to stay away. Such exercises can only happen through the medium of signifiers anyway. That is, the neurotic is so thoroughly a product of language that there is no way out.

The wonderful case of Dora comes to mind here. The infamous 'Lake Scene' is the ultimate comedic-drama: Dora has grown weary of Herr K.'s clumsy attempts to seduce her. He obviously does not get that 'no means no' (incidentally, Dora's father and Freud are of little help to her also). In a last-ditch effort to convince Dora to be his lover, Herr K. drops his bombshell: Frau K. means nothing to him. This declaration signifies the stupidity of Herr K.: Dora never wanted to be his 'one' because her 'one' is Frau K., who he declares is his *nothing*. The one in question is able to mark the freeing of the signifier for the subject, as Frau K. did for Dora in enabling her to ask, without ever articulating the actual words: *what does it mean to be a woman?*

Apophatic discourse and the contemporary neurotic think perhaps that freedom consists in killing the hostage taker. Psychoanalysis sees it differently, and we can repeat Žižek's riff on Wagner here: only the spear that smote you can heal the wound. Hence, our idea of a Stockholm Syndrome when it comes to the position Lacanian psychoanalysis takes on language. The way out of the impasse is to fall in love with what has taken you hostage—signifiers.

Remarks along these lines—about desire, effacement, the real, signifiers—can also be found in Lacan's tenth seminar:

> The bloodstain, whether it's the one that Lady Macbeth tires herself out with or the one that Lautréamont designates with the term intellectual, is impossible to remove because the nature of the signifier is precisely to strive to wipe away a trace. And the more one seeks to wipe out the signifier, to find the trace again, the more the trace insists as a signifier. From which it results that, concerning the relationship with that whereby the *a* manifests itself as the cause of desire, we're always dealing with an ambiguous problematic. (1962–1963 [2014], p. 137)

Indeed, just before these remarks Lacan presents us with what we will call the bug's dilemma, which very neatly encapsulates the topology of neurotic desire. Lacan is telling us a story here, in which a bug acquires some sort of awareness, some sort of ability to represent the space it is wandering around in: a space that happens to be the one-sided surface of a Möbius strip.

> If the insect that wanders along the surface of the Möbius strip forms a representation of the fact that it is a surface, he can believe from one moment to the next that there is another face that he hasn't explored, the face that is always on the back of the face along which he is walking. He can believe in this other side, even though there isn't one, as you know. Without knowing it, he is exploring the only face there is, and yet, *from one moment to the next, it does indeed have a back.* (ibid., p. 136. Emphasis added)

This is only apparently a contradictory statement. In Kant's solutions to the dynamic antinomies (freedom vs. necessity, most notably) there is no contradiction if we make something like a phenomenon/noumenon distinction. In Lacan's terms, a similar contradiction is resolved if we make a distinction between intuition and structure. Just as Kant argued that the contradiction between freedom and necessity could be resolved if we took each to apply to a different realm, the noumenal for freedom, the phenomenal for necessity, here Lacan is saying that the bug's intuition is always right in assuming that there is some other side to the surface it is crawling on, but it is structurally incorrect to say that there is in fact another side.

And so it is with the relationship between language and silence in apophatic discourse. At every moment within language, we have the sense that there must be some sort of absolute silence on the other side of it, some sort of pre- or non-linguistic noiseless, pristine realm. There must be something like the silence of being, before us and without us. This seems like an unavoidably correct and obvious conclusion to make. But what we cannot see, what our experience is not able to direct us towards, is the structurally correct conclusion that there is not one, that the only silence available is not one that is beyond language, but one that is available only within language. That is, the silence we can get is one that actually depends on and assumes the presence of language. The absolute, impossible silence posited by apophatic discourse only takes on its allure because of this structure. This will be the topic of our next chapter: how psychoanalysis calls our attention to and uses in practice this insight about silence: a silence that is produced by, and that can only be, an effect of language. As Lacan says in his *Écrits*:

> Even if it communicates nothing, discourse represents the existence of communication; even if it denies the obvious, it affirms that speech constitutes truth; even if it is destined to deceive, it relies on faith in testimony. Thus the psychoanalyst knows better than anyone else that the point is to figure out to which 'part' of this discourse the significant term is relegated, and this is how he proceeds in the best of cases: he takes the description of an everyday event as a fable addressed as a word to the wise, a long *prosopopeia* as a direction interjection, and, contrariwise, a small slip of the tongue as a highly complex statement, *and even the rest of a silence as the whole lyrical development it stands for.* (1966 [2002], pp. 251–252. Emphasis added)

We're well aware of the status of the real in Lacanian theory, and we're not saying that Lacan is some sort of linguistic idealist (only words exist, there are no things as such). What we are saying is that apophatic discourse and neurotic desire engage in a bit of fetishistic disavowal regarding language: they (and we) know very well that the word is the death of the thing…but all the same…they (and we) continue to dream of obtaining access to the thing we believe is living on unscathed by the effects of language. Silence, in this its imaginarized version, would be one of these things. Or, another way to put the point is to say that apophatic discourse wants to remain a discourse, continuing to use language, just without the signifier's malevolent effects. (For example, to have one's cake and eat it too…) This can give rise to the wish for a cleaner, more just, more precise language which can be uttered and understood without doing any violence to things; or, it can lead to what we think is the only logical conclusion for this view, the Wittgensteinian position that it is better to be silent than to utter what can only be considered nonsense. What Lacan highlights, and even requires us to affirm instead, are the irreversible effects of signifiers on the real. The real has been irreversibly transformed by signifiers: the only solution is to double down on language, as well as the unique space for silence that is carved out within language, and not beyond it. We find this a much more dialectical view of the relationship between language and silence as well.

Going back to our points about sublimation, signifiers, and courtly love poetry, there is something else in Lacanian theory that approaches the status he gave to courtly love poetry, and it is found in Lacan's remarks about what he called feminine *jouissance*. For Lacan, there is a different relationship to language and signifiers involved in feminine sexuation. It is not the case that language is on the masculine side, and silence on the feminine. We think this would overlook the truly dialectical nature of Lacan's view.

While we have been describing a sort of neurotic view of silence as an imaginary object, is this only true of the masculine side of sexuation? Is the other dimension of silence (that is unsayable) part of feminine *jouissance*? There is, after all, something unsayable about it, as Lacan never tires of pointing out. In *Encore* (1972–1973 [1998]) Lacan presents the doctrine of femininity as distinctly feminine *joussiance*. Here he makes a provocation to ***woman*** to speak; that is, to articulate anything about their sexuality, about their *jouissance*, and about their subjectivity. Why specifically the question to ***woman***? Because ***man*** is rendered mute, he cannot say anything. Lacan goes on to discuss this impasse in table of sexuation (Fig. 1.1).

Considering the table, this might be what is expressed in the two arrows, one moving toward the phallic signifier and the other to the signifier of the Other's lack. Or rather, it is in the latter only that we see what we are talking about.

Perhaps the most renowned advocate for reclaiming the pathos of the woman, or more precisely, that of feminine jouissance is Colette Soler in her *What Lacan Said About Women* (2003) who says of the Woman that she

> is the absolute Other is to say that she will not be at all like what could be said about her, that she remains outside the symbolic, and is real in the double sense of what cannot be said, and of what derives jouissance from the non-Phallic. By definition, the absolute Other challenges any possible attribution of qualities to her. (ibid., p. 46)

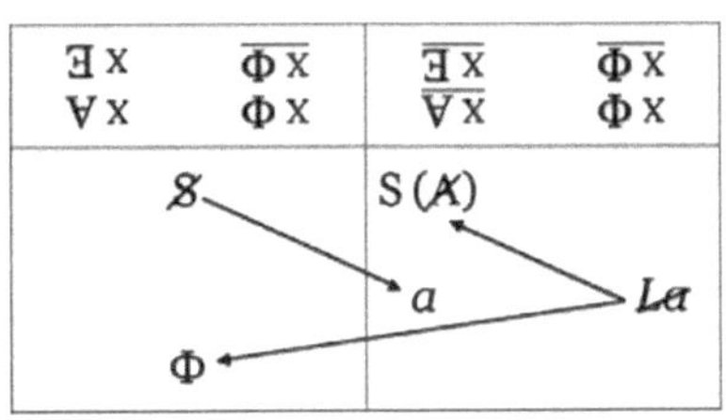

Fig. 1.1 The formula of sexuation

However, Soler goes on to make a compelling claim about the Woman and her structure of being:

> Women, by definition, are originals. They are a race of jouissance.
> What does not exist can, nevertheless, be spoken of. (ibid.)

Wouldn't this be true of silence as well? While there is a struggle with speaking and articulation, this struggle does not seem to have the same qualities as the discursive exercises in apophasis. This could be said to be the feminine position.—what can be said about one's designation to the Phallic structure? And of course, here we must look to Lacan's typology of sexual difference as a way of identifying what is possible to be said with the language that we have got to work with.

On our reading of the formulas of sexuation, the masculine side seeks to find the object a of desire and in thinking that he addresses The Woman, he is actually addressing the cause of desire—he is seeking to make the Woman desire him. The female phallic side (that is, the Woman is between the Phallus and jouissance) is characterized by feminine jouissance, the not-all portion which resists restriction of Phallic identification. She signifies the lack in the Other or as Lacan goes on to purport, *having or being the symptom* (that is, woman as symptom). But of course, not just any symptom, one that is unique, one where feminine jouissance makes the Man (*faire l'homme*). Hence the arrow traversing the binary indicates the 'other side', that which cannot be said—that is the Other which is more Other than itself. And let's not kid ourselves, we are always attempting to articulate this impossible Other, a side which seems to frustrate us so much because of its unsayability.

According to Fink (1997, pp. 106–113) all *jouissance* that exists is Phallic, but the 'other' *jouissance ex-sists*, that is, non-Phallic *jouissance* must be spoken and be allowed to play out in language. So, within the symbolic registers, which we will elaborate upon more fully later, it is the sinthome, the kernel, which gives the condition of the symbolic order coherence and consistency. The sinthome is that which attaches itself to the fundamental fantasy—it is both the consistency and supplement to the three registers (Fig. 1.2).

If language occurs and manifests within this symbolic event, then the masculine and feminine position of speaking and its relationship to the Other is bound by jouissance as either a limit or a surplus. Regardless, it is the unsayability of *jouissance* which allows for a constellation of

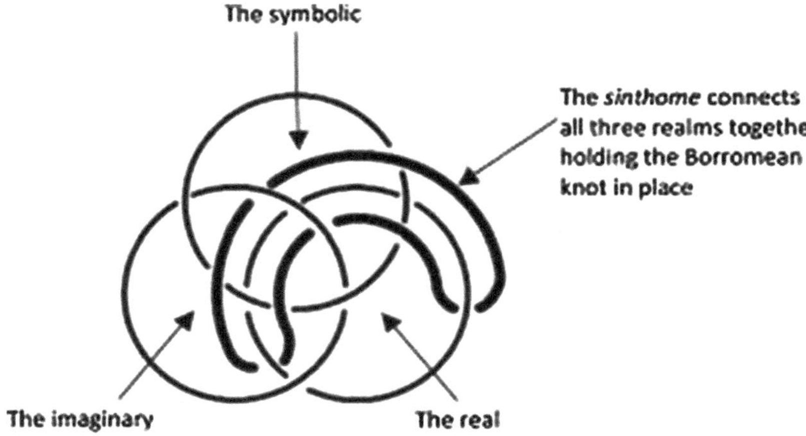

Fig. 1.2 The *Sinthome* in the Borromean knot

language and silence to provide the conditions for desire which emerge as symptoms, which always signify, which always have 'something to say'. However, when the signifier, that which renders the Other as not ineffable because of its signification with/to the Phallus, becomes all too real, we are stunned with not only what to say but how to say it. Here silence covers the chaos of the signifier which is breaking from the chain of signification. In a passage from his fourteenth seminar Lacan refers to the sexual act as what represents silence, in contrast to the constant chattering of the unconscious about sex. What this means is that the object (the voice or some other part of the body), will never be able to signify subjectivity because of its investment in *jouissance*, while the drive, being the sexual act, is invested in the fantasy of impossible structures.

So, what is identified as sayable is bound within the speaking body of a particular binary—either having or being the Phallus or rather, either having or being the symptom as Lacan eventually claimed. The man is moved to know the woman as a unique object in and of herself. And here is the push to *jouissance* and the cause of masculine desire, as Freud points out for us. In this sayability we are left with the lingering conundrum: psychoanalysis never says what a woman is and any attempt to do so is always cautionary. Woman, the not-all of language, is essentially, silent.

There is another aspect of silence in and of the imaginary to be found not only in neurosis but in the forms of psychosis that Lacan was interested in early in his career. We are thinking of his early essay on the sensational case of the Papin sisters, Christine and Lea, who savagely murdered the mother and daughter of the family who employed them as maids. Lacan alludes to a silence that functions in their case that we think qualifies as imaginary, yet in a different sense than the one we have been discussing so far.

A bit of background, first. Resulting from an unloving marriage, both of the sisters were unwanted children. There were suggestions that Christine was sexually abused by her father. Eventually both sisters were placed in an orphanage. By 1929, when Christine was 24 and Lea 21, both sisters had decided to estrange themselves from their mother and were living and working together as maids in the household of the Lancelin family. According to witnesses and acquaintances there was "virtually no verbal communication between the sisters and their employers" (Edwards and Reader 2001, p. 8). As Lacan writes in his essay on them, they were seen by friends and neighbors of the family as model but mysterious servants. Lacan writes that while their masters "seem, strangely, to have lacked any human sympathy, nothing allows us to say that their [the sisters's] own haughty indifference was only a response to this attitude: between the two groups 'one did not speak'. This silence however could not have been empty, even if it was obscure to the actors themselves" (1933 [1988], p. 25).

We're interested in what Lacan is referring to here as a silence that could not have been empty. Remember that Lacan wrote this before he made the well-known distinction between empty and fully speech in his early seminars. It's easy to imagine what an empty silence might be: one that occurs out of boredom or indifference; one that occurs because the parties involved simply have nothing to say to each other…This would not necessarily even be an awkward silence, or an oppressive silence. One can imagine an empty silence in which the individuals involved even get along with each other and like each other. It would be a silence that simply doesn't mean anything: it is not some inscrutable object of desire, it is a silence that just happens, sometimes. *So ist es*!

By contrast, then, is a silence that is not empty necessarily a meaningful silence? Not at all. Instead what we think Lacan is pointing to here is something like the silence of a structure, or silence as a structure. It is a silence that reigns for structural reasons. The structure we have in mind is the familial and social structure of tensions that shaped and exacerbated the *folie a deux* of the sisters; a structure that extended to encompass, fatally, the family they were working for.

One normally associates structure with the symbolic in Lacanian theory, but this is not entirely correct. There are complex imaginary structures. Who can correctly count how many parties are involved in the mirror stage? (We think the answer is… at least four, maybe five?) In this case, there was no symbolization of the relationship between the daughter and the mother who were murdered, and on the other hand of the sisters' relationship to the two of them. The mother/daughter dyad in the family they lived with was considered by the Papin sisters to be a duplicate of their own such that, in typically imaginary fashion, this duo was seen as a rival and threat to their own unity. (That is, in the imaginary order, it is all you or me, us or them…)

What we see in this case—and what no doubt intrigued Lacan about it—is an extreme case of silent mirroring. (Lacan wrote his essay on the Papin sisters in 1933, three years before he delivered his first paper on the mirror stage.) There was no overt hostility—in fact, according to the records of the time, outwardly, the mistress treated the sisters seemingly well for the time. However, it did become apparent during the trial that the mistress did express some minor criticality towards the sisters from time to time. What is more relevant is the relationship the sisters had with their biological mother, whom they eventually came to renounce and disown. The tensions which ensued from this decision, and their relationship, transferred to the Lancelin family and this was signified specifically in the name they used for Mrs. Lancelin (Edwards and Reader 2001, p. 10). Edwards and Reader quote the psychiatrist assigned to them as saying that they called Mme Lancelin *maman*, "not, needless to say, to her face" that add, yet when their mother visited them in prison they called *her* Madame… As they conclude, this is "one of the many bizarre mirrorings with which…this case is riddled" (ibid., p. 10). One psychiatric expert asked to examine the case described the girls as "… since they behaved like wild animals, they must be treated like savages and wild animals" (ibid., p. 14).

Following the murders, while the sisters did not deny their guilt, they simply for a while refused to elaborate on why they murdered so viciously. This makes complete sense: what was there to say about it? In addition, they were always guilty and never denied it. The murder itself was particularly gruesome: they had gouged out the eyes of both the mother and daughter with their fingers, then proceeded to bludgeon and stab them to death. After the murder the sisters were found upstairs in the bedroom, in bed together, naked.

During the trial Christine, however, said something rather interesting. "*Mon crime est assez grand pour que je dise ce qui est*" [My crime is great enough for me to tell the truth about it]. Perhaps we are dealing with a situation here similar to what Lacan found in his thesis on the case of Aimée, the frustrated actress who stalked and eventually stabbed her rival. Lacan famously called this a crime of *auto-punition*—self-punishment, an attack on the self—and he wanted to account for the improvement in mental health that occurred after such crimes were committed. However, the crime of the Papin sisters can be read in another way: as one that broke the silence which inhabited them and oppressed them. That is, in the absence of symbolization an attack was launched on the organs of the imaginary *par excellence*, the eyes. Not seeing, being blind, is like a silence in the visual realm: a silence of the visible. Or a silence which makes something visible. It seems as though Lacan thinks of silence not as way into the knowledge of the Real, but rather as a semblant. That is, it is insufficient on its own as carrying an effect. Grigg (1997, n.p.) offers a succinct formula for the semblant:

> [F]or Lacan 'semblant' carries the connotation of being seductive and therefore deceptive. We believe in semblants, or rather we opt for a semblant over the real because semblants are a means of satisfaction or a way of avoiding unpleasure; when a semblant collapses, anxiety emerges. It fills a lack by coming to the place where something should be but isn't, and where its lack produces a negative affect of some sort, but focusing on anxiety. Semblants are a form of substitution of something that provides a source of satisfaction for another object that would cause anxiety. The general formula is
>
> $$\frac{A}{\varphi}$$

The import of apophasis is propagated in a variety of ways as we have seen—certainly as a communicative strategy of silence, as filling a lack. What apophasis does is make the unsayable neither the opposite nor something separate from language. Rather the unsayable is revealed in and through the action of language (such action is a wrestling with language itself) such that it becomes vital to its sustenance. But these 'successes', when language manages to negate itself, are also linguistic failures, and this is where there are some risks involved for apophasis.

Negation is one of the fundamental properties of language, yet a danger to it because it is recursive, as Wittgenstein (1922 [1981]) reminds us—language should do to itself what it does to everything else: Negate. Hence, according to Wittgenstein, we ought to simply shut up when we have nothing to say or there is nothing else to be said (if only language was that straight-forward!). Ironically, silence will carry the discussion further than any words can. Here silence is not one dimensional, and negation is not empty, which is what we have been arguing thus far. Both can be tactical and discursive, a form of malaise, experiential, comical, horrifyingly violent, and a way to struggle with the language we have to work with.

We don't intend our argument against apophasis to be in the realm of the psychological: those who live in glass houses shouldn't throw stones! What we do mean is that Lacan is giving us a structural and topological insight into a particular impasse that is intrinsic to language—and it is an important perspective on what seems like an impossibility regarding an unreachable other-side. In the next chapter we will discuss how silence plays a role in the formation of this structure, which is a critical component of the split subject. The capacity of this subject to be silent even turns out to be what Lacan calls the core of this subject—its essential capacity, its Aristotelean energeon. From this perspective, silence is an enabling condition, rather than an impossible object. And this is what we would like to develop more fully. The point is that silence is not to be revered, we are not to stand in awe of it: silence is to be used, strategically. We wish to take silence out of the realm of the sacred and into the mundane. In our Chapter 3 we will consider different strategic uses of silence in literature and music but before this we would like to think about how silence is a condition which enables.

References

Beckett, S. (1954 [1982]). *Waiting for Godot: A Tragedy in Two Acts.* New York: Grove Press.

Dinouart, A. (1771). *L'art de se taire, principalement en matière de religion.* Paris: Petite Bibliothèque Payot.

Dolar, M. (2006). *The Voice and Nothing More.* Cambridge: MIT Press.

Edwards, R., & Reader, K. (2001). *The Papin Sisters.* Oxford: Oxford University Press.

Fink, B. (1997). *The Lacanian Subject: Between Language and Jouissance*. Princeton: Princeton University Press.

Franke, W. (2007a). *On What Cannot Be Said: Apophatic Discourses in Philosophy, Religion, Literature, and the Arts. Volume 1. Classic Formulations*. Notre Dame, IN: Notre Dame Press.

Franke, W. (2007b). *On What Cannot Be Said: Apophatic Discourses in Philosophy, Religion, Literature, and the Arts. Volume 2. Modern and Contemporary Transformations*. Notre Dame, IN: Notre Dame Press.

Franke, W. (2014). *A Philosophy of the Unsayable*. Notre Dame, IN: Notre Dame Press.

Grigg, R. (1997). The Concept of Semblant in Lacan's Teaching. *Lacan.com*. Accessed from http://www.lacan.com/griggblog.html.

Kojève, A. (1949 [1969]). *Introduction to the Reading of Hegel: Lectures on the Phenomenology of Spirit* (J. Nichols, Trans.). Ithaca: Cornell University Press.

La Rochefoucauld, F. (1959). *Maxims*. New York: Penguin Books.

Lacan, J. (1933 [1988]). Motives of Paranoid Crime: The Crime of the Papin Sisters. *Critical Texts, 5*, 7–11.

Lacan, J. (1953–1954 [1991]). *Seminar I: Freud's Papers on Technique* (J.-A. Miller, Ed.). Cambridge: Cambridge University Press.

Lacan, J. (1959–1960 [1992]). *Seminar VII: The Ethics of Psychoanalysis*. New York: W. W. Norton.

Lacan, J. (1961–1962 [2002]). *Seminar IX: Identification* (C. Gallagher, Trans.). London: Karnac.

Lacan, J. (1962–1963 [2014]). *Seminar X: Anxiety* (J.-A. Miller, Ed.). Cambridge: Polity.

Lacan, J. (1966 [2002]). *Écrits* (B. Fink, Trans.). New York: W. W. Norton.

Lacan, J. (1972–1973 [1998]). *Seminar XX: Encore—On Feminine Sexuality, the Limits of Love and Knowledge* (B. Fink, Trans.). London and New York: W. W. Norton.

Milner, J.-C. (1995). *L'Œuvre claire, Lacan, la science, la philosophie*. Paris: Seuil.

Nasio, J.-D. (1987). *Le silence en psychanalyse*. Paris: Payot.

Taylor, C. (2016). *The Language Animal: The Full Shape of the Human Linguistic Capacity*. Cambridge: Harvard University Press.

Wittgenstein, L. (1922 [1981]). *Tractatus Logico-Philosophicus* (C. K. Ogden, Trans.). New York and London: Routledge.

CHAPTER 2

Silence, the Enabling Condition

> Concerning the factors of silence, solitude and darkness, we can only say that they are actually elements in the production of the infantile anxiety from which the majority of human beings have never become quite free—Freud, *The Uncanny*, p. 252.

Abstract This chapter discusses the various ways in which silence is used in psychoanalytic practice and theory. It considers arguments from Reik as well as Lacan and others about the importance of using silence in the clinic, and then turns to a discussion of how Lacan gave the experience of silence a crucial role in his theory of subject-formation.

Keywords Lacan · Reik · Nasio · Milner (Jean-Claude) · Fleiss · Silence · Analyst's silence · *tacere* · *silere* · Skepticism · Demand · Drive · Graph of desire

Although he hardly seems to mention it, we're convinced that silence is in fact a major Lacanian concept. Furthermore, Lacan develops a unique and crucially important ethics of silence, one that responds to a shift in the status of silence that we will associate later with the emergence of the natural sciences. In this chapter we want to begin by discussing the importance of silence for Lacan in clinical practice, which will lead us to Lacan's views on the role silence plays in the very formation of the subject. In contrast to the mode of silence discussed in the previous chapter,

E. Pluth and C. Zeiher, *On Silence*, The Palgrave Lacan Series,
https://doi.org/10.1007/978-3-030-28147-2_2

here we are seeing a silence that is used, that is part and parcel of the symbolic itself and not located on its other side.

It is useful at this point to think about how silence is 'accomplished'. The Lacanian analyst Juan-David Nasio edited a volume on silence and psychoanalysis and chose to begin it, appropriately, with a text by Theodor Reik from 1926 entitled *In the Beginning was Silence*. Reik's essay is quite a find, and we are inclined to call it proto-Lacanian. Nasio believes it is the first essay in the history of psychoanalysis to "sustain the positive technical value of silence on the part of the psychoanalyst" (1987, p. 13). In his essay Reik emphasizes the importance of language use in psychanalysis (already a unique perspective for the time), and the importance of paying attention to linguistic facts. Aware that many people in the early days of psychoanalysis were sceptical about whether symptoms could be dealt with by words alone, he points out that these same people, as children, believed in the magical powers of words, and that even into adulthood they can continue to be moved and enthused by them. But in his opinion, it would be incorrect to ally psychoanalysis with the use of words alone. He adds that it would be "more exact to say that psychoanalysis proves the power of words *and that of silence as well*" (Reik in Nasio [1987, p. 22]. Emphasis added).

At the rare moments when Freud himself brought up the topic of silence, his points fell into two main categories: silence was either an indicator of repression (that is, it was a sign that repression was happening in real time), or it was a feature of the workings of the death drive. Repression itself, Freud wrote in 1912, is a process that "is accomplished in silence". And when describing what happens when an analysand fails to produce any associations after a manifestation of the unconscious, Freud explains that this was usually an indicator that some specific thought about the analyst had occurred. If the analyst interprets in this direction, "the obstacle is surmounted or, at least, the absence of associations is transformed into a refusal to speak" (Nasio 1987, p. 277. Translated from original French). Even Reik speaks of the analysand's silences primarily as something that is like a 'zone' the analysand continually wishes to enter, one in which the active repression of associations can continue to take place—what more could an analysand want?

But in a point that, as far as we know, Freud never touched on, Reik discusses not only the anlaysand's silence but the *analyst's*. (One does get the impression, rightly or wrongly, that as an analyst Freud himself was rather chatty and quick to interject…) When the analysand hesitates to say something, or actively doesn't want to say it, silence from the analyst can acquire what Reik describes as an "active power" that is able to "makes transparent the little nothings of the conversation" (ibid.). Silence on the part of the analyst "possesses a force that pulls the patient along, makes him progress, and draws him towards depths greater than those that he had envisioned" (ibid., p. 26). Why would this be the case? Reik observes that "when we pronounce them, words have a different value than when we think them in our verbal representations. The articulated word has a retroactive effect on the one who speaks. *The analyst's silence intensifies this reaction: it acts like an amplifier*" (ibid., p. 26. Emphasis added). In other words, silence plays an important role in creating the very conditions in which the unconscious can be attended to. That is, silence is critical in making sure that the fundamental psychoanalytic rule—say whatever comes to mind—is followed. In fact, it even seems to make a sort dialectical process possible.

> Gradually, the psychoanalyst's silence changes meaning for the patient. Something came to mind that he does not wish to say, or that is difficult for him to say. He speaks of this and that, feeling quite clearly that he is avoiding what wants to be expressed. Then he falls silent, like the psychoanalyst. [...] The patient [...] begins to speak of secondary things, of trifles. But the thought that he repressed comes back. It wants to be expressed, it forces itself through the wall of silence by imposition, by interfering with any other chain of ideas. It is possible that then the patient turns towards the psychoanalyst and asks for help, but the latter preserves his silence, as if this was the only normal attitude: without any concern for the social world that avoids such embarrassing silences in conversation. (ibid., pp. 25–26)

The only obligation one has as an analysand is simply to speak. Reik observes that this obligation entails the production of words *and silences*, and not words alone. This is what gets the analytic process going. Lacanian psychoanalysis has made this stratagem into a cornerstone of its practice, of course. Indeed, Lacan's own psychoanalyst, Loewenstein, was known for his silences and his lack of interventions (Roudinesco 1994, p. 231).

Nasio observes that the literature on silence in psychoanalysis is nevertheless rather thin (Reik makes the same point in his essay). But silence remains a

> fundamental theoretical entity: it remains, among all the diverse human manifestations, that which expresses the best, in the purest fashion, the dense and compact structure, without noise nor speech, of our own unconscious. The famous Lacanian assertion 'the unconscious is structured like a language' does not at all mean that the unconscious is made up of speeches or sounds. The unconscious is not a language even if it is born thanks to language. No, the structure of psychic reality — what we call the unconscious or the Id, knowledge or jouissance; or again the Symbolic, Imaginary, and Real – remains a perfectly mute structure, without any resonance, closer to the flatness of letters written on marble than to words spoken from the mouth. (in Nasio 1987, pp. 9–10)

While Nasio is certainly right to say that the unconscious is not *a* language (nor is it *language*), a point many have been wrong about, might Nasio be going too far when he writes that the unconscious is not "made up of speeches or sounds" either?[1] If it isn't, how can the unconscious be the locus where "it speaks" as Lacan always said it was? Of course, Nasio is aware of this basic Lacanian point. What Nasio is pointing out, rather, is the silence of some of the key structures and concepts of psychoanalysis: the drives, enjoyment, the real, we can add the imaginary...and Nasio himself even wants to include the symbolic. To say these orders or registers are silent is not, of course, to say that they have nothing to do with language, but rather that they are hard to articulate and further, to decipher. But in spite of the difficulties in handling language, curiously, Nasio claims that it is actually silence that expresses the unconscious in the best way.

It is here that we think about what is accomplished in silence. In his books on clinical practice Bruce Fink (1997) touches on the uses of silence not in explicit terms perhaps, but at least implicitly when he writes about the importance of punctuation and scansion. These techniques have everything to do with silence and its relation to speech; they are a way of handling speech by acting with silence. Advising his readers against an over-emphasis on interpretation—"interpretation has virtually no beneficial effect until the analysand has formulated a true demand for

[1] This kind of claim is typical of Nasio. In another work he mentions that the unconscious does not exist *except* in the clinic. We can see the point he's trying to make—it is usually only in the clinic that its appearances are actively attended to—but it strikes us as not theoretically convincing and even philosophically suspect to say that only the clinic provides the context for the unconscious to exist.

analysis"—Fink hastens to add that "this does not mean the analyst need say nothing at all during the preliminary meetings; rather, it means that his or her interventions should consist of 'punctuations' of the patient's speech, the analyst proffering a meaningful 'Huh?!' or simply repeating one or more of the patient's words or garbled sounds" (Fink 1997, pp. 14–15). Legends about the silence of Lacanian analysts are widespread, and perhaps Fink does not wish to perpetuate the stereotype. But we think that, as Fink describes it, these punctuations of the analysand's speech are essentially silences, the kind of silences essential to analytic work that Reik was writing about.

But the silence of the Lacanian analyst need not be always understood in terms of actual silence. It is not so much (or not only, or not just) that she is literally silent so much as she is an unconventional interlocutor, not engaging in the typical back-and-forth of conversation expected within the social bond. In fact, Reik's essay already pointed this out: the psychoanalyst does not observe the etiquette and niceties of ordinary conversation. Lacanian psychoanalysis goes further than Reik did in its theoretical justification for this practice. Whether actually remaining silent or not there are profound reasons for why the Lacanian analyst is encouraged to practice silences: its purpose is to move the position or function of the "subject-supposed-to-know" away from the person of the analyst and towards analysand's unconscious. This is no easy feat, and it is a further elaboration of Reik's idea that silence serves as an amplifier for the unconscious. So, if silence is in fact an amplifier for the unconscious, we could say that Lacanian analysts are the ten-foot Marshall stacks of silence. They are professionally silent.

But let us take a step back: what, or rather who, is the subject-supposed-to-know? Perhaps even before the first meetings, perhaps only gradually, an analysand will put the analyst in the position of someone who possesses the knowledge about her symptom that is required in order to cure her. When put into this position what the analyst says can take on a transformative power. This is the position Freud's patients put him in during the period when his interpretations alone were able to bring about instantaneous effects: the analysand's symptoms would disappear just like that. Yet, as Freud himself pointed out, what happened in such cases was not unlike what happens in hypnosis, and if psychoanalysis had stuck with such a practice, it would have been nothing more than a sub-category of the power of suggestion. Freud's move away from hypnosis in order to develop psychoanalysis proper is well known. Lacan, it could be argued, thought yet another move away from a practice anywhere close to the hypnosis/suggestion spectrum was necessary, and we think that silence is an important part of this move. (After all, one would have to be an awfully talented hypnotist to hypnotize somebody in silence!) The analyst perhaps cannot avoid being put into the position of the subject-supposed-to-know, and being put into this position may even be a necessary step towards the establishment of a properly analytic discourse—for bringing about what Fink referred to as a true demand for analysis. But the Lacanian *pragmatics of silence* (Dolar 2006) is able to bring about a shift in the location of this function from the person of the analyst to the unconscious of the analysand itself. This is the crux of transference.

The point of the Lacanian analyst's (relative, not total) silence when using punctuation then, as Fink describes it, is to attune the analysand herself to manifestations of her unconscious as they happen, to that "Other desire" that outs itself in her speech. Punctuating the analysand's speech with repetitions and echoes (or silences) shifts the analysand's attention, as it were, away from the analyst's interpretations toward the very material of his or her own speech, toward what is said in it that would otherwise slip by unnoticed. Šumič-Riha explicates this nicely when she says that in analysis, silence speaks as a testimony to the voice:

> Thus, it could be said that, in the analysis, we are dealing with the overlapping of two silences: the analysand's, which is an eloquent silence, a silence that 'talks' without knowing it, and the analyst's silence, which is an act that makes it possible for the analysand to hear the 'voice' of silence, that silence of the unconscious desire and/or drives of whose 'talking' he - or she is unaware and which nevertheless agitate him or her. It is in this sense that it could be said that the analysis becomes the place where the impossible-real can be exposed. (2004, p. 20)

Even Lacan's development of the variable length session can be understood as a use of silence in the clinic. Fink (1997) discusses this under the heading of "scansion," a word that usually means paying attention not to meaning but to sound and rhythm. *Scanding* as a psychoanalytic technique is something that calls attention to the silences between signifiers, we could say. In the variable length session, the analysand's speech is punctuated (*scanded*) by an interruption, a cut, as it is commonly called among Lacanians. Surprise is in fact an important feature or effect of scanding, as Fink notes that "[w]hen the analyst suddenly ends a session, he or she may accentuate the surprise the analysand has just been expressing, or introduce the element of surprise through scansion, leaving the analysand wondering what it was the analyst heard that he or she had not heard, wondering what unconscious thought had been manifesting itself" (1997, p. 17). Scanding is a silent rupture, an agitation of words.

In *Variations of the Standard Treatment* from 1958 Lacan himself discusses the analyst's silence directly. In a section with the heading "What the psychoanalyst must know: how to ignore what he knows" (1957–1958 [2017], p. 290) he writes that the psychoanalyst acts as a rather unique support for the analysand's speech.

> For that is what he does for the subject's speech, even by simply welcoming it, as I showed earlier, with an attentive silence. For this silence implies speech, as we see in the expression 'to keep silent' which, speaking of the analyst's silence, means not only that he makes no noise but that he keeps quiet *instead* of responding. (Lacan 1966, pp. 290–291)

When Lacan wrote theses lines it was at a time in his work when the determining and overlooked importance of the symbolic register was first and foremost in his mind. Lacan's reference to "true speech" in the same essay is indicative of this. Silence in the clinic, as Lacan is describing it here, is a crucial part of moving speech away from its imaginary dimension towards what he thinks is its properly symbolic one. And, as we said above, it is a move that Lacan seems to think is crucial for creating the right conditions for the psychoanalytic cure to take place. Significantly, this move is accomplished with the help of a pragmatics of silence.

The analyst is described here as a support of the "subject's speech"—the analysand's speech, to be clear—and in some sense any conversation partner serves as such a support. Think of all the times we say to our conversation partners things like "you understand?" "you know?": the other assents, and we feel somewhat more assured that our words are hitting their mark.[2] Lacan is suggesting here that in the clinical setting, because of the basic structure(s) governing conversation, even

[2]This is different from what Jakobson called phatic communication, communication without real content, as when we ask "hey, what's up?" without expecting a real answer.

the analyst's *silence* functions as such a support. The analyst's silence is bound up with speech and this is the case not just because silence implies listening—we could even say, especially *not* because silence implies listening—but because, Lacan emphasizes, silence already and necessarily takes on the value of a *response* in the analytic context. "Keeping quiet *instead* of responding," as Lacan puts it, makes the analyst's silence count as a choice, an action, an intervention, and an important move in the analytic process itself. In fact, we could modify what Lacan says to make the implicit conclusion even more clear: keeping quiet *is* a response. It could be said that the analyst's job is to intentionally remain silent: she is not silent because she simply has nothing to say, or is bored. Rather her silence is meant to provoke the analysand into transference. This might be different from the analysand's silence, who falls into silence from time to time. A way to think about this—and we discuss this more in Chapter 3—is that there exists a difference between active (the analyst's) silence, that is silence which is perhaps a drive against one's will, and passive (the analysand's) silence, is more of an appeal to the Other for something.

When he refers to a "keeping quiet instead of responding" Lacan is leaning on a distinction that was important in Pyrrhonean skepticism between *tacere* and *silere*. We will be making much of this in what follows. Lacan takes this distinction up explicitly years later, in his fourteenth seminar, and it ends up playing an important role in his theory of subject formation. In a discussion of this distinction in Nasio's collection, *tacere* is described as actively, purposely keeping silent, while *silere* is just accidentally, casually being silent. It can be thought of as a distinction between activity and passivity, then: or, in terms of intentional acts and unintentional ones. In English, the word *tacit* derives from *tacere*: that which is implied in speech without actually being said. In French the verb *se taire* (to keep or stay quiet, to shut up) derives from *tacere*. In Pyrrhonian scepticism *tacere* even made up part of an entire ethic according to which one should keep silent *when one should have or could have done otherwise*. When one is called upon or expected to speak, one doesn't: Sextus Empiricus says that this is not simply or primarily in order to avoid uttering what are inevitably untruths. Instead, when confronted with multiple positions and views and uncertainties, the skeptic chooses not to speak, which shows that he is not bothered by uncertainty and is not overhasty in trying to resolve it. This is part of an effort to attain *ataraxia*—a state of serenity or calmness.

> When a skeptic chooses to remain silent, he isn't searching for a comfortable refuge in the midst of doubt or for a means of avoiding error. To the contrary, he is only reflecting the state of balance of his soul when confronted with uncertain representations and submitted to equal contrary forces. (McKerrow 1966, p. 25)

We're not sure whether silence in the clinic reflects the balance of the analyst's soul (we have our doubts about that), but isn't it the case that part of what motivates the Lacanian analyst's silence is a concern to avoid over-hasty interpretations, to move psychoanalysis away from suggestion? And more so, doesn't such silence in fact solicit speech, which is the obligation of being in analysis? In Barthes' discussion of this distinction in his seminar from 1977–1978, *The Neutral*, the difference is glossed this way: *silere* is a near-mystical silence, like the silence of nature, the stillness of things, but *tacere* is the silence of speech, a symbolic silence or a silence in and of the symbolic.

Arguably, a practice of silence ended up overtaking Lacan's seminar itself. We're thinking of what are referred to as the notorious "silent seminars" of the late Lacan. Elizabeth Roudinesco claims that after a minor car accident with mathematician Pierre Soury, in which Lacan was not visibly injured, he nevertheless at the beginning of the seminar immediately following it "for the first time loses his ability to speak before a silent and stupefied audience" (Roudinesco 1994, p. 641, as well as her very similar account in *Jacques Lacan*, 1997, p. 515). The seminar she is referring to is for the year 1978–1979, *Topology and Time*, and transcripts for the first session are indeed odd. Lacan does speak, *pace* Roudinesco, but barely. At the end Lacan even says, "There, I've spoken for an hour. Thank you for your attention". It takes no more than a few minutes to read the entire transcript for this session, and it is dominated by the presentation of topological figures of Möbius strips and Borromean knots. What little commentary there is from Lacan is preoccupied with discussing these figures. Things go downhill from there. In the next session of that year's seminar he makes an erroneous point about Borromean knots, which is pointed out to him by someone in the audience. Lacan apologizes, says he is confused, and stops the session short. It goes on like this through several more sessions. One gets the sense that he knows when it is time to shut up. Roudinesco also reproduces some testimonies from some of Lacan's analysands during this period, who noticed a change in how Lacan's silences occurred and were practiced. Nevertheless, it seems that Lacan's analysands, inevitably, struggled to read theses silences as interventions. Perhaps they were in mourning for the Lacan that once was.

While Roudinesco medicalizes the late Lacan (after 1978, remember that Lacan died in 1981), we should consider Jean-Claude Milner's alternative thesis that Lacan adopted a practice of silence for rigorous, doctrinal reasons. The last chapter of Milner's 1995 *The Clear Œuvre*, entitled "The Deconstruction," is about the collapse of what he calls the two 'classicisms' that had characterized Lacan's thinking prior to his silent seminars. Milner entertains the hypothesis that the Lacan of the silent seminars ultimately embraced the view we attributed to Wittgenstein's ethic in the previous chapter: what cannot be spoken of is something that one must remain silent about. However, if this were true, it would mean that Lacan broke radically with his previous views.

Prior to this period there were two sorts of ethics guiding Lacanian practice, expressed in two similar but also different phrases. One was the idea that the truth can only be *mi-dire*, half-said, and the other that psychoanalysis cultivates the art of *bien dire*, of saying it well, despite impossibilities and impasses. Milner considers that Lacan's recourse to Borromean knots in his seminars signifies his conclusion that these two options or ethics ultimately failed. Thus, "with every showing [*monstration par monstration*], the knot hinders *mi-dire* as a way to get to *bien dire*" (ibid.). Why is this? Here we see what Milner thinks the Lacanian conclusion might have been:

> ...but the impasses of *mi-dire* and the inaccessibility of *bien dire* are an abolition of the unconscious. If silence is not only required, but also possible ('you must remain silent, thus you can'), it is because the truth does not speak and the unconscious does not exist. There is no Freudian thing". (ibid., p. 170)

Here, what Milner is saying is that Lacan considered truth not only to be something untouchable or unattainable by knowledge but that knowledge is not even transmissible.

In what he calls Lacan's 'second classicism' and the renunciation of his earlier views on science, transmissibility of knowledge, mathemes and so on, Milner claims that it is Lacan's hyper-structuralism which accounts for this second turn. That is, for Milner, the late Lacan is characterized by his preference for mathematicising, for formulas and topology as a way of transmitting his 'philosophy' or more pertinently, anti-philosophy as a formalization of psychoanalysis. In a 2008 (Peden and Milner) interview about *Cahiers pour l'analyse* Milner refers to this transmission as particularized by mathematical properties in spite of structural linguistics not using mathematics at all. But contrary to this displacement Lacan uses this form—complete reduction to matheme—as his most transmissible, although he offers a caution in *Encore* about his deployment and mobilization of mathematics (ibid., p. 110): "they are not transmitted without the help of language, and that's what makes the whole thing shaky." Milner furthers Lacan's apprehension in contending that his reliance on this procedure is for the most part a modernist project which allows as Adrian Johnston says (2015, p. 146):

> The sub-title of Milner's *L'Œuvre claire*, in which Lacan's name is linked to science as well as philosophy ('Lacan, *la science, la philosophie*') might be recalled here: just as scientific equations such as 'E = mc2' ultimately do nothing more than descriptively encircle facets of a universe with no transcendent, metaphysical Other or Elsewhere—the sheer, brute givenness of immanent materiality in its inexplicable contingency is science's one-and-only Ground Zero, that which it represents without adding any supplementary meaning or guarantee of necessary significance—so, too, do Lacan's mathemes, equally as meaningless as the mathematical formulas of physics, reflect the baseless base of subjectivity's structures as beneath or beyond the spheres of sense.

But according to Milner this is only true of the second classicism in Lacan's thinking, a period in which the matheme, and not linguistics dominated.

In contrast to what we were discussing in the previous chapter, with these practices of silence it is obvious that we are squarely in the domain of silences that are part of the symbolic. These are silences that are communicative, as opposed to the silence that we've argued functions in an imaginary register—that impossible silence that is the target of apophatic discourse, an inaccessible object of desire. In Lacanian psychoanalysis silence acts, and is used, as a destabilizing or alienating communicative manoeuvre on the part of the analyst, for both parties involved. Clearly, this is a silence that is part of language, the kind of silence that we call, with Dolar, a "pragmatics of silence," one that is "firmly rooted in silence as part of discourse, symbolic silence" (Dolar 2006, p. 155).

Françoise Fontaneau in her *L'ethique du silence* (1999) also calls this a silence that "can be an interpretive act, making up part of the art of *se taire*" (p. 136).

Silence is valued in psychoanalysis not because it is the pure other to language, not because it takes us beyond language, but because it is thoroughly within language, yet in an uncanny way. It attunes us to the various happenings in language we might not otherwise hear (such as manifestations of the unconscious, a slip of the tongue after which we wished we had remained silent!). The fact that silence relies upon sound is so obvious and yet constantly over-looked. It is precisely because the Lacanian subject is an effect of signifiers that silence is one of the best ways to shake the subject up. A strategic silence is as good a way as any to hystericize the subject, which as Fink argues is an important step in getting a psychoanalysis going (1997, p. 131). Lacanian psychoanalysis utilizes a silence that jars, one that highlights gaps and splits. It is not a healing, restorative silence at all, but a disruptive one, and one that echoes or repeats the very creation of the split subject. Šumič-Riha (2004) takes this a bit further by suggesting that silence itself can be thought of as being split, that it speaks, talks to us, as either as *taceo* or *sileo*. This is a silence that can be said to speak.

Are we saying then that silence is a signifier? Well, yes and no. If signifiers are defined by their differences from other signifiers in the chain of signification then silence stands out for its distinct difference from all signifiers as such. If this is the case, how can it qualify as one itself, particularly when silence is not an object to be counted? Or, does this make silence into some sort of transcendental signifier, the condition *sine qua non* for any other signifier? Or is it, in structuralist fashion, some sort of degree-zero signifier or phoneme? If we go in this direction with silence and the symbolic, we have to be careful. Thinking of silence as something that precedes signifiers would be going in the direction of the imaginarized silence treasured by apophatic discourse. We think psychoanalytic discourse is oriented in an entirely different direction.

Psychoanalysis focuses on and uses a silence that is an effect of language, what Marx might call a "post-festum" silence (where language would be the party only after which silence follows), a silence that is only possible with and after language. Giorgio Agamben is on to a similar point, although in a slightly different register, when he writes that "the unsayable is a genuinely linguistic category" (1998, p. 35). And Žižek too when he writes that "voice and silence relate as figure and ground:

silence is not (as one would be prone to think) the ground against which the figure of the voice emerges; quite the contrary, the reverberating sound itself provides the ground that renders visible the figures of silence" (1996, p. 93).

Whether 'practices' of silence are always communicative or not is a point we will consider in the next chapter. John Cage thought that his work doesn't and shouldn't have the intention of communicating anything at all. In fact, he contends that this ought to be the intention of all art: to say something would simply signal the end of it. This could be Cage's discovery, then: the creation of a composition that "says nothing" as he put it "I have nothing to say and I am saying it" (1952, *Lectures on Nothing*). To *say* nothing is like a degree zero of communication, a pure/empty form of communication.

But let us return to the connection between the Lacanian subject and silence. Silence turns out to have formative importance for the subject. It is easy to repeat with Lacan that the subject is an effect of language, of signifiers. Part of what is important about this thesis is that it is an anti-phenomenological move: it figures the subject not as self-consciousness, not as a synthesis, not as a unity, not as a thinker, not as an ego. It avoids psychologism. We have here maybe two fundamental slogans for Lacanian theory: neither psychologize nor 'phenomenologize'! It is also easy to focus on the importance of the Lacanian idea that language has effects in the real, on the body, and that this is why the drives are the way they are. But a companion thesis of Lacan's idea that we are deeply shaped by language is that this shaping does not occur without an equal contribution from silences—because these too are an intrinsic part of the speaking beings we are. Language carves out a space for a kind of silence that becomes formative, a post-linguistic silence with a novel status.

In other words, it is not enough to think about subject formation in terms of language acquisition, to think about the preexistence of the symbolic, the precedence of signifiers, the codicil tattooed on someone's head that Lacan liked to refer to, the one in which someone's destiny is written... all of these familiar Lacanian points about the importance of language do not suffice to account for the formation of the subject. It's the silences that accompany them, that punctuate them, that are the missing ingredient that makes the subject, the drives, and the unconscious into what they are. This discussion will ultimately move us toward the last aspect of silence we want to cover, the silence in/of the real. But before that, since silence turns out to be an integral part of the symbolic, we need to reconsider or highlight a few things that might otherwise go unnoticed: the importance not only of the Other's speech (a central concept in Lacan's dictum that the unconscious is the discourse of the Other) but of the Other's silence as well.

We are particularly interested in how this is addressed in a passage from his seminar *The Logic of Fantasy* from 1966–1967. The *Ècrits* had been published a few months prior, and Lacan is expanding on his formula for the drive from the graph of desire: Barred-S, lozenge, D, situated in the graph's upper right-hand corner. At the time he was trying to counter the rather interesting critique someone made about his lack of attention to the importance of silence in the *Ècrits*. The formula for the drive, Lacan claims in this passage, means exactly that the drive only begins when demand shuts up.

He reiterates his argument that what makes psychoanalysis distinct from other disciplines and discourses is its handling of the subject of science, and that this subject has a particular structure which is due to the fact of language. But language not only structures this subject: this subject is also distinctive, in contrast to the subjects of other sciences (animals, chemicals, stars), for something beyond its ability to speak. What this subject's unique capacity is, what Lacan refers to as its "energion" in Aristotle's sense (we'll take this to mean its defining activity), is, surprisingly, its ability to be quiet, to *se taire*. Of course, the subjects of other sciences are also rather quiet (the planets, the stars, the universe do not speak…). At this point that Lacan explicitly leans on the distinction in Pyrrhonean skepticism between *silere* and *tacere*. To reiterate, *silere* is just merely happening to be silent (as is the case for nature) while *taceo* is silence as a deliberate action (and this is what Lacan says is the defining ability of the subject of psychoanalysis). It is well worth quoting the passage from the *Logic of Fantasy* at some length:

> Structure, I've been teaching…is the fact that the subject is a fact of language. […]. The subject thus designated is the one to which we generally attribute the function of speech. But it sets itself apart by introducing a mode of being that is its specific energy: I mean in the Aristotelian sense of the term energy. This mode is the act in which it keeps quiet (*se tait*) – *tacere* is not *silere*. This is, however, a fuzzy distinction. To write, as someone has, that one looks for any allusion to silence in my *Ecrits* in vain is ridiculous. When I wrote the formula for the drive at the upper right hand of the graph as S◊D, that means that it is when demand shuts up (*se tait*) that the drive begins. But if I did not speak at all about silence it is precisely because *sileo* is not *taceo*. The act of keeping quiet (*se taire*) does not free

> the subject from language. Even if the essence of the Subject reaches its climax in this act. [...]. Keeping quiet remains heavy with an enigma that the animal world has oppressed us with for a long time. We find traces of this only in phobias now, but, let's remember that for a long time the gods were placed in the same spot too. (1966–1967, p. 95)

The act of keeping quiet does not free the subject from language: This is exactly what silence as *taceo*, not *silere*, is about. *Silere* is the accidental, de facto perhaps, silence of the real and imaginary. *Taceo* is a silence that is the stuff of the symbolic. But why does *taceo* become the subject's *energion*?

We have already discussed the importance of silence in the clinic. But Lacan does something a bit surprising here and calls *tacere*, the ability to keep quiet, the subject's supreme act, its Aristotelian *energion*. Following Lacan's lead, considering the formula of the drive more carefully—S◊D–is the key to figuring out why he makes this claim. This will take some digging back into earlier seminars.

Let's start with Lacan's statement that this formula means that it is when demand shuts up (*se taire*) that the drive begins. The drives begin with a silence, then: and a very particular silence, not silence as *silere* but as *tacere*. That is, with an active silence, or, we can say, a silence in and of the symbolic. The formula S◊D was created by Lacan when he was thinking about the exchange of needs and demands between children and parents. This is the crucible in which desire and the drives are formed, and it turns out that while Lacanian theories of subject-formation usually focus on language and signifiers, the formation of the subject does not occur without what is for all intents and purposes the silence of the Other: the absence of a signifier, a non-response. The location of S◊D on the graph of desire should be taken as an illustrate this. The point on the graph where we find S◊D repeats at the level of the unconscious what appears directly below it—the Other as the treasure-trove of signifiers (Fig. 2.1).

S◊D can be considered a subset of those signifiers in the treasure-trove, ones that make up the "signifiers of demand". A sort of mini-Other: more concrete, perhaps, and certainly more involved in verbal and libidinal exchanges.[3]

[3]We would like to point out that we think that the graph of desire is actually a bit misnamed. It is not exactly a graph, and it is about much more than desire. Here it needs to be understood chronologically or diachronically as well as synchronically. The precursors

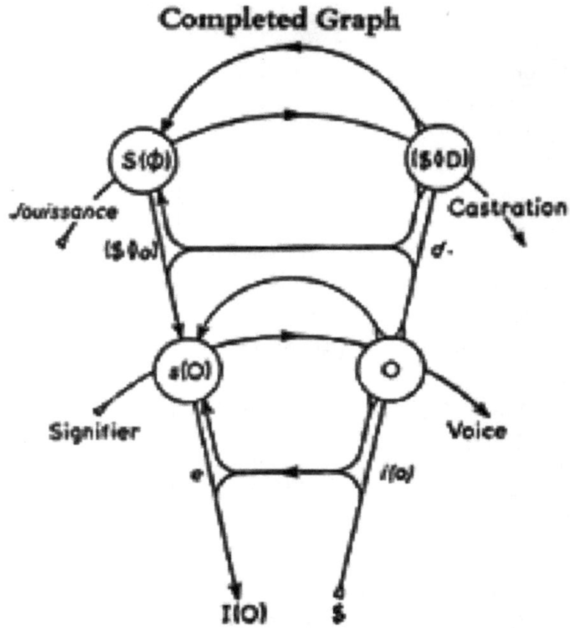

Fig. 2.1 The graph of desire

Of course, it is also very important that this is the first place in the graph where the barred-S appears. A first version of the split subject is placed here (repeated by the split subject in the formula for fantasy). This is assuming one is supposed to "read" subject formation on the graph from the bottom right to the bottom left, following the Delta vector, what Lacan calls in seminar five the line or vector of "need" intersecting the signifying chain, the Other, and resulting in all of the consequences that follow (1957–1958 [2017], p. 60). This also follows what the "explanation of the schemas" tells us at the end of the published seminar, in which the basic schema is described thusly:

to the graph are absolutely necessary for developing an understanding of what is on the graph in its final form, and because the graph is about more than the formation of desire, it includes an account of the formation of the drives, of fantasy, of the ego, and the superego.

> What comes next represents the discourse's intention for you, which also has to be indicated inasmuch as the discourse is not detached from the concrete individuality who is uttering it. The duality of the subject operates in an 'intersubjective conjunction'. From its first cry, the newborn baby connects with the mother from whom it will acquire the use of the signifying chain. That's essentially the schema. (1957–1958 [2017], p. 488)

Hence, the first point of contact between the two lines needs to be portrayed as the Other itself, the existence of language as a set of signifiers. The second point of contact, to the left of that point or circle, is where we see the retroactive pinning down of a meaning for signifiers that were encountered initially but remained enigmatic. It is only after an encounter with the treasure trove (or battery) of signifiers that the signifiers first encountered gain some meaning, at least by means of clarifying differentiations. It is as if what Lacan is saying here is that without the whole of language, discrete and fragmented bits of language—signifiers—would never be anything more than enigmas. Indeed, it is important to remember that the whole graph begins to be constructed when Lacan is trying to make a point about the structure of puns and witticisms, which he thinks have a structure similar to that of any manifestation of the unconscious. It is rather easy to see how retroactivity is important for any such analysis. Jokes and retroactivity must go hand in hand as it is the creation of a surprising and unanticipated meaning, for signifiers/conditions that were assumed to be a certain way, or were just objectively unclear, uncertain.

The silence at stake here is both a verbal absence and an absence of speech. The distinction between these two absences are important to realise. We can say that silence too is a libidinal investment in the drive. The perceived absence of the Other in demand is also silent Other. But we want here to call attention to the idea that it is more than this, it is a literal knotting of demands and Lacan speaks to this when he refers to the analysts as "an adequate apprehension of the effect of a silent saying" (1974–1975, n.p.). In the clinic silence cuts directly affecting anxiety (or jouissance) in analysand if it effective and timely. How might it do this? Let us start with the drives. Freud early on considered "stoppage" as an expression of resistance directed against verbalization from which silence occurred (1912, p. 101).

> The stoppage can invariably be removed by an assurance that he is being dominated at the moment by an association which is concerned with the doctor himself or with something connected to him. As soon as this explanation is given, the stoppage is removed, or the situation changes from one in which associations fail into one in which they are being kept back.

This is a conscious silence, or a silence made conscious was understood by Freud as interrupting or unconsciously resisting free association. So, silence was an ambiguous form in stopping the drive. However, later in 1926, he reconsidered this idea, saying that silence as resistance is a way into exploring the repressed drives. Interestingly however, he did not offer any technique to handle the patient's silence as he largely considered it a defence against drive. However, in 1949, Fleiss theorized that speech emanates from a pre-genital zone which corresponds to a quality of silence. Certainly, he attests that the speech-act assists in overcoming this resistance through releasing the various closures in the erotogenic zones, these being the oral, anal and genital. The function of silence for Fleiss was to maintain repression of the erotic wishes.

Regarding silence as resistance against oral-erotic wishes, Fleiss claims that this resembles a kind of mutism in that the subject expresses nothing, his point being that there is a resistance to struggle with language. He claims that such resistance is a will towards negation, that is, to make oneself absent. In the clinical setting Fleiss understood this as the most repressive, infantile and narcissistic of silences because in the will-to-silence, the subject is dependent on the response of the other, the analyst. This kind of orally repressed silence is one which Fleiss says has the function of maintaining the ego.

Fleiss also discusses resistance against anal-erotic wishes is more of a bodily manifestation, where through the fragment of thought, the patient experiences rage, hostility, tenseness and guilt. This kind of silence is characterized not so much by an absence of words, but rather, by enunciation. The subject knows that he or she is thinking, but can't see the point in speaking—the affective body is speaking for them (We offer an example of this in Chapter 3 when thinking about Claudel's *The Hostage*). Fleiss sees this as a kind of helpless silence, one in which silence is in some ways both involuntary and ambivalent. As Fliess says in Nasio:

> The child acquires language at the same time as *sphincterian* control of the anus and urethra, and this new possibility of *exteriority* present since birth, will become of primary importance. The discharge of tension, which can

> no longer be brought about by physical means, will be able to make itself by speech. The activity of speaking gets substituted for the activity *of bodily orifices. Words, themselves, become substitutes for corporeal substances.* (in Nasio 1987, p. 73)

Fleiss's silence as resistance against phallic-erotic wishes is characterised as a defence against the oedipal impulse. This is kind of resistance aimed at jouissance which is complicated by castration anxiety. However, the silence which ensues is a kind of wager where the subject attempts to bargain on the basis of silence. Resultant alienation is noted by Freud when he remarks that when the analysand is confronted with the analyst not returning love, the analysand becomes disenchanted and tempted to end analysis as a procedure which fails to give love a go. The refusal of love is complimented by the refusal of words: this is an identification with the aggressor.

A comment from Seminar IV, before Lacan starts developing the graph of desire as such, sheds some further light on how this formula is connected to silence. Lacan was working on the distinctions between frustration, castration, and privation at the time, as well as their different statuses (symbolic, imaginary, real). His reflections on these points are what led him to develop the graph of desire in the first place. The important point for us is what Lacan has to say about what happens when the demand for love is frustrated. When this happens, the (real) objects that normally satisfy needs take on a different status: they become charged with a symbolic force, and become signs of the Other's love. This brings about a new sort of action on the part of the subject. We'll call this a first step in the formation of the drives, and it is significant for being one of the first moments in which the real for the child gets overwritten, affected, by the symbolic. A passage also worth quoting at length:

> Let's start with the support of the first love relation, the mother insofar as she is the object of the call, and thus an object as absent as she is present. On the one hand there is what she gives, which are signs of love, and as such are only that – that is, anything else about them beyond being signs of love is cancelled out. On the other hand there are objects of need, which she presents to the child in the form of her breasts. Don't you see that between the two there is both an equilibrium and a compensation at work? Every time love is frustrated, it is compensated for by a satisfaction of need. When the mother is missing to the child who calls for her he clings to her breast, and this breast becomes more significant than ever.

> As long as he has it in his mouth, and is satisfying himself with it, on the one hand the child cannot be separated from the mother, and on the other hand she lets him be nourished, rested, and satisfied. The satisfaction of need is here compensation for the frustration of love, and it begins at the same time to become, I'd almost say, its alibi.
> The prevalent value that the object, here the breast, or the nipple, takes on, is founded on this fact: a real object functions as part of the beloved object, it takes its signification as symbolic, and the drive is addressed to a real object as part of the symbolic object, it becomes a real object as part of the symbolic object. On this basis we can understand oral absorption and its so called regressive mechanism, which can happen in any amorous relation. From the moment when a real object that satisfied a real need is able to become an element of a symbolic object, any other object able to satisfy a real need can come to be put in its place, and first and foremost this object that is already symbolised, but also partially materialized, that is speech. (1956–1957 [1994], pp. 174–175)

In the wake of the absent Other the ordinary and familiar objects of need receive a different libidinal charge: objects of need, when they become available again after the Other's absence, are no longer objects of need but signs of love. Lacan is already touching on what he would later think of in terms of excess and *jouissance*. In fact, we even have here the basic outline of object a. But what light does this shed on the idea that the drive begins when demand shuts up? On the basis of this passage we can connect the 'shutting up' of demand with frustration. It is in the wake of the frustration of the demand for a sign of love—the silence of the Other—that objects of need get transformed into drive-objects.

This requires an interesting amendment to Lacan's famous idea that signifiers introduce lack. Perhaps we can say that this capacity of signifiers is a necessary but not sufficient condition for the creation of the subject. A sufficient condition, we suggest, would be the Other's silence.

Language and speech themselves get caught up in the mechanism Lacan describes in seminar four, and become something other than mere means of communication. It is very rare to see Lacan consider speech itself as a libidinal object. (The voice, yes, but never speech. Should we think that speech and voice are the same thing? Dolar, of course, warns against this slippage!) But he suggests that speech itself is the sort of object that can take on the role of an 'alibi'; a real object that serves as compensation for a frustrated symbolic demand for love. We believe that this reference to a libidinal investment in speech itself, as a reaction to frustration, is very important for understanding the nature of the drives and the role that silence plays in them. In other words, this is the key point that leads Lacan to develop the formula for demand, S◊D.

But we are not quite there in setting up our problem with silence yet—we also need to include the notion of the Other's desire. There is an intermediate stage in the graph's development at which this is accounted for. Lacan typically characterizes it in terms of a question: what do you want, a *Che Vuoi?*, emerging from the place of the Other. He variously describes this question as a question that the Other asks of the child, and as a question the child has about what the Other wants. Given how desire is itself for Lacan a dialectic, and nothing without that, this intermixing of subject and Other in the question is entirely appropriate, and there is no need for us to determine which comes first. The important point is that desire just is a questioning, an enigma, in all directions, we might say.

We think that it the Other's silence, as a mode of the Other's absence, is one crucial way in which the Other's desire is encountered. This makes the Other into one who does not respond not only at the level of needs (by absences) but also at the level of language. This effectively shuts up demand, putting into play the mechanism Lacan described earlier, in which the objects of need become drive objects. Lacan makes similar remarks in the next years' seminar:

> What do we see, then, on this horizon that is rendered opaque by the obstacle of the Other's desire? Insofar as the Other no longer responds, the subject is referred back to his own demand, he is placed in a certain relationship to his own demand which is designated here by the symbol of the little lozenge that I explained to you last time. Here, 'big A is not answering' [*'grand A ne repond plus*], a very famous sentence with different initials. (1957–1958 [1994], pp. 451–452)

The subject being referred back to its own demand: this is one way that the formula for the drive could be read, it is what barred-S/lozenge/D is describing. This is a movement, an activity, that at the same time seems to be at the very origin of the subject: hence Lacan's interest in calling it the subject's energion in Aristotle's sense: energion means activity, after all.

We are now ready to consider the canonical explanation of the formula from *Subversion of the Subject* in *Écrits*:

> The drive is what becomes of demand when the subject vanishes from it. It goes without saying that demand also disappears, except that the cut remains, for the latter remains present in what distinguishes the drive from the organic function it inhabits: namely, its grammatical artifice, so manifest in the reversals of its articulation with respect to both source and object. (1966, p. 816)

Lacan then goes on to discuss erogenous zones. This is rather elusive as an explanation of the 'notation' for the drive, even by Lacanian standards. And minimalistic: this must be the *least* Lacan says about any part of the graph. Is Lacan referring to his earlier discussions of frustration obliquely here, when he mentions the subject vanishing from demand? When the demand for love is frustrated by absence, this could indeed be thought of already as a vanishing of the subject, though not yet quite the same as the vanishing that characterizes the subject of fantasy and desire… And it would also seem that one could equally well say that the Other has vanished at this point. The demand disappears, and the cut remains… What we have then is a subject attached to former objects of need, now in a drive-like fashion. No longer demanding love and recognition from the other, but engaged, precisely because of a cut, in procuring satisfaction in a compensatory way (as an alibi). It's this kind of drive-like attachment and activity that makes up the subject's own *energion*. That's why Lacan describes *taceo* in such terms. And without the Other's silence as well, this does not take place.

The passage from seminar fourteen on *taceo* is one that others working on Lacan and silence have been drawn to. Franzini, in a case study in Nasio's volume on silence, claims that these remarks have to be understood as an elaboration on the formula: *there is no sexual act*. This was a formula Lacan spent time on in this seminar, and it was a precursor to his later claim that there is no sexual relationship. What does silence have to do with the sexual act? As Franzini puts it, "[w]e will see that Lacan makes of the sexual act a representative of silence" (1987, p. 128). Here we take Franzini to mean that the sexual act becomes a placeholder for silence, and in this respect the idea here is along the same lines as the later idea that the unconscious is involved in a writing of the otherwise non-existent sexual relationship. There is some analogy between the status of silence and the status of the not-all sexual relation. More specifically, like the non-rapport, silence warns against the illusion of wholeness, fullness or total presence. In fact, Badiou is very suspicious of any ethic in which silence is elevated to such a status, maintaining that such a testimony of silence should be refused as a legitimate signifier (Badiou 1992, p. 195.) Šumič-Riha claims that silence, especially for Lacan, is a way *in* to the problem of language:

> Lacan succeeded in writing silence, not, of course, as a sign for the impossibility of saying, but, on the contrary, as a mere semblant-instrument whose function is precisely to make it possible for the analysand to take it as the cause of his or her desire and to come to terms with his or her desire. (2004, p. 18)

The fourth chapter of Fonteneau's book, *The Ethics of Silence* (1999) opens with a discussion of this passage and draws a similar connection between silence and sexuality. She reads the *taceo/silere* distinction as an active/passive distinction as well, in which taceo (the root of *se taire*, again) is taken to mean actively keeping quiet, or even actively keeping *something* quiet.[4] This allows Fontaneau to read silence as a type of act that manifests "the subject of speech" in a particularly strong way. And she also reads this type of silence as a manifestation of the unconscious, as a sort of background manifestation of it out of which other symptoms may be built—it is a "silence always already there" (ibid., p. 127). This is what allows her to link silence to the death drive and sexuality. The unconscious, as Lacan notes, is a lot of chatter, a sort of discourse that "roars, grumbles, coos, and complains," and always about sex. Yet this unconscious sex-obsessed chatter is also seen as the way in which the unconscious effectively shuts up about the sexual non-relation (here, what he is calling the sexual act) for which its endless kvetching about sex is trying to compensate.

We should add that in psychoanalysis silence actually runs in two directions. In *Variations* Lacan writes:

> It is to the extent that the analyst manages to silence the intermediate discourse in himself, in order to open himself up to the chain of true speech, that he can interpolate his revelatory interpretation. (1966, p. 293)

[4]Nasio even lines *taceo* up with repression and *sileo* with forclusion. "Is there a silence proper to repression and another distinct from it, proper to forclusion? My hypothesis is the following: whereas the silence of repression implies that something already there, already existing, has been repressed, forclusion's silence expresses, on the contrary, the abolution of what had to or should have appeared but didn't. This distinction comes close to

The analyst's silence has value not only as a response then and is not only directed towards the analysand, but is also a move toward the analyst's own internal monologue. Silencing her own discourse also acts as a check on the analyst's tendencies to interpret, understand, and assume the tendency of the analyst's, as Fink puts it, to be focused on what the analysand might mean instead of "what the analysand actually says" (1997, p. 24) literally.

In 1967 Lacan makes reference to the *mi-dire* of silence as only being half terrifying as language inevitably sutures the subject into a 'science' of psychoanalysis. That is, silence renders a subject-effect and affirms the dependence on language.

> The eternal silence of whatever it may be, whatever you like...only terrifies us about half as much as it used to. This is because science appears to us, to the common consciousness, as a knowledge that refuses to depend on language: and we overlook that it also refuses to depend on the Subject. It is not the case that science does without the subject: it removes the subject from language. I mean it expels it from language. It creates formulas in a language rid of the subject. It begins with a prohibition on the subject-effect of language. This has one important result: it demonstrates that the subject is only an effect of language, and an empty effect at that. From this moment on it is surrounded by the void. That is, the subject appears as a pure structure of language. This is what the discovery of the unconscious is all about. [...]. The unconscious is a moment when a phrase speaks in the place of the subject of pure language, a phrase we are never sure who uttered. The unconscious, with what we can certainly call its scientific status, since it originates with the fact of science...the unconscious is the fact that the subject, rejected from the symbolic, reappears in the real, and it presents in the real what we see being made by the history of science. [...].

Such a suturing can be thought of as a practice of silence (as well as unsayability) which we will now turn our attention to.

the one Lacan takes up from the ancients between the silence of *taceo* and the silence of *sileo*. *Taceo* means to silence oneself, to silence in oneself something existing; whereas *sileo* signifies the void of something that never came to be. In distinction to the active silence of repression corresponding to *taceo*, there is that of the forclusive abolution coming from *sileo*" (p. 140).

References

Agamben, G. (1998). *Homo Sacer: Sovereign Power and Bare Life*. Palo Alto, CA: Stanford University Press.

Badiou, A. (1992). Conférence sur la soustraction. In *Conditions*. London: Bloomsbury.

Cage, J. (1952). *Silence: Lectures and Writings*. Middletown: Wesleyan University Press.

Dolar, M. (2006). *The Voice and Nothing More*. Cambridge: MIT Press.

Fink, B. (1997). *A Clinical Introduction to Lacanian Psychoanalysis Theory and Technique*. Cambridge: Harvard University Press.

Franzini, A. (1987). Une aphonie éloquente. In Sous la direction de J.-D. Nasio, *Le silence en psychanalyse* (pp. 123–134). Paris: Petite Bibliothèque Payot.

Freud, S. (1912). The Dynamics of Transference. In *The Standard Edition of the Complete Psychological Works of Sigmund Freud*. London: Hogarth.

Johnston, A. (2015). This Philosophy Which Is Not One: Jean-Claude Milner, Alain Badiou, and Lacanian Antiphilosophy. *S-Journal, 3*, 137–158.

Lacan, J. (1956–1957 [1994]). *Livre IV: La relation d'objet et les structures freudiennes* (J.-A. Miller, Ed.). Paris: Seuil.

Lacan, J. (1957–1958 [2017]). *Seminar V: Formations of the Unconscious* (R. Grigg, Trans.). Hoboken, NJ: Wiley.

Lacan, J. (1966 [2002]). *Écrits* (B. Fink, Trans.). New York: W. W. Norton.

Lacan, J. (1966–1967). *La logique du fantasme*. Unpublished typescript.

Lacan, J. (1974–1975). *Seminar XXII: R.S.I.* (C. Gallagher, Trans.). Unofficial Edition.

McKerrow, R. B. (1966). *The Works of Thomas Nashe*. London: Blackwell.

Nasio, J.-D. (1987). *Le silence en psychanalyse*. Paris: Payot.

Roudinesco, E. (1994). *Histoire de la psychoanalyse en France II*. Paris: Fayard.

Roudinesco, E. (1997). *Jacques Lacan* (B. Bray, Trans.). New York: Columbia University Press.

Šumič-Riha, J. (2004). Testimony and the Real: Testimony Between the Impossibility and Obligation. *Parallax, 10*(1), 17–29.

Žižek, S. (1996). I Hear You with My Eyes. In S. Žižek & R. Salecl (Eds.), *Gaze and Voice as Love Objects*. Durham: Duke University Press.

CHAPTER 3

Silence as Practice

For the only way one can speak of nothing is to speak of it as though it were something. (Beckett, *Watt*, 1953, p. 50)

Are you looking for the silent man? (Melville, *Bartleby*, 1853, p. 62)
No. (Claudel, *The Hostage*, 1917 [2009])

Abstract This chapter looks at the 'writing' and portrayal of silence in literature and music. We closely consider Beckett, Melville and Claudel as well as John Cage's infamous silent composition, *4′33″* as varying ways in which silence is invoked and grappled with.

Keywords Lacan · Cage (John) · Beckett · Melville · Claudel · Active silence · Literary silence · *tacere* · *silere* · Speechlessness · Jankélévitch · Unsayability · Drive · Anxiety · *4′33″* · *The Calmative* · *Bartleby* · *The Hostage*

We've considered uses of silence in the clinic, and Lacan's views on the formative importance not only of language but of silence for the subject. We want to begin this chapter with the tricky relationship between silence and unsayability, which is going to be important for working out the ethics and pragmatics of silence that will be the topic of this and our final chapter. At first glance experiences and encounters with silence and unsayability are not that dissimilar, and may appear to involve one

E. Pluth and C. Zeiher, *On Silence*, The Palgrave Lacan Series,
https://doi.org/10.1007/978-3-030-28147-2_3

and the same thing: any distinction between them might seem trivial or hair-splitting. For our argument however, there is an important distinction between them in which drive activities play a crucial role. If the drive begins when demand shuts up, then silence as a choice, or an act, is intimately connected to the absence or failure of signifiers, especially as encountered in the Other's absences and the Other's desire. Yet as Lacan adds in *Logic of Fantasy* (1966–1967), falling silent in reaction to these encounters still does not liberate the subject from language; at the same time, he claims that the essence of the subject also culminates in the act of falling silent. Being silent does not result in wholeness then; in fact, Lacan is suggesting that the very essence of the split subject can be found in its unceasing efforts to be silent within language, to be silent *with* language (and not simply and entirely against it, beyond it, or outside of it). This struggle is what we are thinking of under the heading of unsayability. Wishing to encounter silence and an encounter with the unsayable are two different things, then: the latter is a struggle with speaking, within language, whereas the pursuit of silence as such can entail a rejection of language altogether, and a desire to efface the work signifiers have already done. The *tacere/silere* distinction is again helpful here. The unsayable, the struggle between language and silence, falls on the side of *tacere*. Wrestling with speaking, as we shall see, is however not at all unconnected to silence. It is useful to revisit Nasio's distinction between these two structural dimensions:

> If we follow schematically the historical evolution of the theme of silence in psychoanalytic reflection, one notices first of all that the distinction that we've just made between the structural silence of the drives (*sileo*) and that of an unspoken speech (keeping quiet, *taceo*), is already manifest in the rare passages in the Freudian oeuvre that refer to it. On the one hand Freud always insists on the necessity of thinking repression, and more particularly the death drive, as a process anchored in the soil of mutism ('… the process proper to repression is accomplished in silence'); on the other, he seems preoccupied with the practical problem raised by silent patients. However, the works of the first disciples of Freud se penchant almost exclusively on this last, technical aspect of the silence of analysands – *taceo* – to the determinant of its structural dimension – *sileo*. (1987, p. 11)

When faced with the lack within language, there are many ways to react to it—certainly one is a repressive force as Freud claimed. Another is the position Karl Abraham called *logorrhea*, which we mentioned in

Chapter 1. One can talk and talk and talk and, in the end, have said nothing. This is one way to handle the anxiety-producing qualities of silence, and this entails an over-valuing of language. Another way is what occurs under the heading of what we are calling the unsayable. For example, at a funeral one tends to be silent, usually as a mark of respect or because one is consumed by grief. Conversely, we have all been in social situations where we would love nothing more than to tell someone to just shut-up… but instead we keep silent out of good manners! We have also all said things to only regret it, wishing that we had remained silent instead. In the event of an unexpected traumatic event, we tend to be affectively orientated, and struggle to find the right language to convey an overwhelming experience. During such traumatic times we experience the failure of words, their inability to capture anguish. In such scenarios this is how the anguish of silence as also a struggle to speak can be thought. We want to identify this experience of unsayability as a drive-like activity that involves wrestling with language, one in which, as Lacan suggested, language itself becomes a libidinal object. Unsayability is a linguistic phenomenon in which there is an effort to express or react, whereas passively being silent (*silere*, not *tacere*) is closer to a desire to remain reverentially silent, language be damned.

With these points in mind we will here discuss some further uses of silence and encounters with unsayability, this time in literary and artistic texts, including selected passages from Melville's *Bartleby*, Beckett's *The Calmative* and Claudel's *The Hostage*. We will also consider Cage's *4'33"* 'silent' composition. By employing these examples what we will explore is how a struggle and an absence of speech is handled and thought. That is, if we take silence to be a practice, which we do, how might the very concept of it be present or make itself known to us?

But to return to how apophatic discourse handles these matters, consider what Jankélévitch has to tell us about the practice of silence. When he writes that "…language appears so secondary, so unconvincing, so miserably inefficacious" (1996, p. 549). Jankélévitch is expressing a profound attachment to lived experience, in which the objects that language speaks about eclipse language itself. This anti-linguistic sentiment is in line with apophatic discourse, equating or situating truth with the lack of language. Following his mentor Bergson, Jankélévitch claims that it is not what one believes, says, or writes but what one *does* (and also what one chooses not to do) that matters: "Practice what you preach, or better yet practice without preaching. Such was the harsh wisdom of

Tolstoy" (ibid.). Since, according to Jankélévitch's dystopian vision of language—language's ultimate failure to capture the full extent of our anguish and our continued imprisonment in it[1]—that is, language only matters when it is fully subordinated to actions, when actions precede or trump what is said. Here language only parrots what has already been done. One may as well be silent whenever engaging in any form of activity, for it is the action that matters most:

> That's it - to be committed, and nothing else. Not to give lectures on commitment, nor to conjugate the verb, nor to commit oneself to commit oneself, as men of letters do, but really to commit oneself by an immediate and primary act, by an effective and drastic act, by a serious act of the whole person; not to adhere half-heartedly but to convert passionately to the truth, that is to say, with one's entire soul, like Plato's liberated captives. (ibid., p. 550)

Although the act itself is not unconditionally privileged by Jankélévitch (who alerts us to the dissatisfaction it may lead to), nevertheless for him the act of refusal in particular embodies a moral principal. In spite of the uncertainty of their effects, these acts are an important part of enacting a truth one cannot otherwise say. For Jankélévitch refusal is a life event; it is also a form of unsayability from which silence emanates.

What leads to Jankélévitch's claim was his view that the Holocaust was an event about which he must remain silent (that is, he has no choice but to) since the horror itself is and will always be, unsayable. Try as one might there are literally no words which could capture the full extent of the Holocaust and it is not a case of simply falling silent out of remembrance. Jankélévitch does not talk about the Holocaust as such, but rather refers to it as an event which is impossible for it to be adequately talked or written about—the event itself exceeds the linguistic turn. He contends that although we can address the effects of the event itself,

[1]It is worth noting that although they were contemporaries, Lacan never mentions Jankélévitch in his seminars. There is only one mention of his father and Freudian scholar, Samuel Jankélévitch in the EPEL index of proper names. Certainly, Jankélévitch had a sympathy for psychoanalysis, and there were some resonances between him and Lacan regarding the problem of language and what can be said, but it seems that they simply did not travel within the same intellectual circles.

such as death, memory, displacement, trauma and so on, the event of the Holocaust itself is unable to spoken about. He eventually goes further to suggest that because of this, forgiveness is not possible because of such unsayability. His writings about the Holocaust focus on the inability of language to capture the acts of horror (and even contends that the desire to try and articulate what cannot be spoken in the end about is nothing more than an empty liberal desire). Here we think that this is a precise engagement with unsayability as falling within *silere*, not *taceo*.

We think that Melville's character of Bartleby is a good example of *taceo* as active silence. In contrast to Jankélévitch's position, Bartleby's mantra, 'I would prefer not to' nicely demonstrates the futility and impossibility of attempts to embrace an imagined, absolute silence. Bartleby's is what we are calling an active silence, and it presents us with a case of dealing with the unsayable. His exclusive repetition of one phrase emphasizes his silence in a way that the total silence urged by Jankélévitch does not. His repetition of the phrase is in fact what makes his silence into a *taceo*, not a *silere*: it is what makes his subject-position a force to be reckoned with, its peculiar ability to resist being found in the fact that his repetition marks his silence and works to signify his refusal. His silence is not passive, rather it is a way of not surrendering to his conditions. We can easily imagine what a passive silence looks like, and how some forms of silent resistance are simply no resistance at all…but Bartleby's silence does not at all fall into this submissive category.

Set in mid nineteenth century New York's Wall Street, Bartleby is hired as a scrivener or law clerk who actively refuses the rat race he is thrust into. He does so by remaining mostly silent and inactive, repeating the phrase 'I would prefer not to' in response to requests and even polite questions from his colleagues. However, Bartleby had not always been like this; as his employer states he "did an extraordinary quantity of writing… but he wrote silently, palely, mechanically" (1853, p. 16). All this changes when his employer summons Bartleby to continue with his work and 'I would prefer not to' is the singular and from then on repeated reply which his employer comes to expect: "Of course, from behind the screen the usual answer, 'I prefer not to' was sure to come…" (ibid., p. 28). The minimalism of this phrase provokes an excess of affect in his employer, ranging from outrage to expressions of sheer perplexity. He attempts many times to reason with Bartleby, to get him to explain his refusal:

> The next morning came.
>
> "Bartleby," said I, gently calling to him behind the screen.
>
> No reply.
>
> "Bartleby," said I, in a still gentler tone, "come here; I am not going to ask you to do anything you would prefer not to do -- I simply wish to speak to you."
>
> Upon this he noiselessly slid into view.
>
> "Will you tell me, Bartleby, where you were born?"
>
> "I would prefer not to."
>
> "Will you tell me anything about yourself?"
>
> "I would prefer not to."
>
> "But what reasonable objection can you have to speak to me? I feel friendly towards you."
>
> He did not look at me while I spoke, but kept his glance fixed upon my bust of Cicero, which as I then sat, was directly behind me, some six inches above my head.
>
> "What is your answer, Bartleby?" said I, after waiting a considerable time for a reply, during which his countenance remained immovable, only there was the faintest conceivable tremor of the white attenuated mouth.

Here Bartleby's response is ironic in that his refusal is itself his answer:

> "At present I prefer to give no answer," he said, and retired into his hermitage.

After much effort, the narrator couldn't do more than to get Bartleby to give a slightly different version of his mantra. Then, after no longer even working there, Bartleby still refuses to leave the office. His 'preference' causes increasing anguish for his employer because of its utter ambiguity: when asked whether he would like to undertake some other task in the office instead of being a scrivener he says "I would not like it at all; though, as I said before, I am not particular".

In addition to working on a whaling vessel, Melville himself also worked in boring offices and experienced the stultifying effects of bureaucracy. *Bartleby* was also written in the wake of hostile criticisms of *Moby-Dick*. Melville had been accused of violating the rules of fiction for including first-hand, naturalistic descriptions of whaling. Today such criticism strikes us as off the mark, and *Moby-Dick* is taken to be symbolic of the insignificance of man in face of nature's power. In its way *Bartleby* continues this theme, with capitalism taking nature's place. Melville's message is clear: we cannot expect our desires to be satisfied, let alone transcended, from neither nature nor capitalism.

Bartleby is an interesting and ambiguous character and it is useful to consider his subjective position as one of melancholia—he has no interest in the life-drive and yet is strangely resilient in his state of subjective suspension. This affords him an agency of sorts where he seems to enjoy tormenting himself and his loss of ego. But even more than this, Bartleby's subjective position allows us to take Melville's novella as a critique of post-industrial capitalism. Implicit in Bartleby's refusal is a liberation in the realization that there is not necessarily a nature of man or of the natural order outside of capitalism. Bartleby stays put with the anguish of this realization. He doesn't, for example, go to India to seek a transcendental mystical experience in compensation for his dissatisfaction, nor does he fully integrate himself into the capitalist project of ongoing production, consumption and recognition (as his employer would certainly prefer). He simply refuses. And stoically so! He suffers in silence—a nevertheless active one. And in doing so, his silence effectively exposes not only the frustration of his employer and colleagues but also the absurdity of the office context.

Bartleby wills nothing specific to take place and yet he is doing something by virtue of the fact that his refusal has an effect. He is not explicitly telling others to leave him alone or to be quiet amongst themselves; he simply wishes not to engage with their chatter. Of course, this doesn't happen as his colleagues continually urge him to speak! Initially experiencing him as rude and odd, they eventually become annoyed and frustrated with his dismissal of their attempts at engagement. Yes, Bartleby responds to questions and requests, not always consistently but certainly reluctantly. So, his speech is a strange will to his silence, and although essentially a desire to be left alone by others, it ends up being a call for his colleagues to respond—this is an effect that characterizes his active silence. Although silence can be an obsessive attempt to efface the signifier's effects, as we discussed in Chapter 1, Bartleby's relation to silence sustains a signifying phrase that does two important things: it both hystericizes the other subjects and resists desire. Let us look at how in more detail.

We have to admit it would be possible to read 'I would prefer not to' as the pursuit of an impossible silence, that is, a hystericizing force, as an instance of apophatic discourse in which language is marking its own inability to signify. Bartleby is, after all, speaking. However, we think that it is through the repetition of his holophrastic signifier that he remains silent. Thus, we can say that he practices his unique silence in order to speak: that his silence only is what it is because he in fact says (and offers variations on) 'I would prefer not to'. Because his silence is articulated, punctuated, it forces his colleagues to respond. Because Bartleby does minimally signify, his interlocutors (and us as readers) are driven to look for the meaning behind his resistance.

In this respect Bartleby's position hystericizes other subjects, and we think it does so effectively because it gives a precise and limited function to silence—echoing the point we made in the previous chapter about the role of the Other's non-response in the formation of the subject. Bartleby is an outrageously sad comic who sustains a logic of negation which is obedient to speech. But it is also a logic which has an enigmatic force: in driving his colleagues to respond to his silence, he ends up placing the (unanswerable) question, *Che Vuoi?*, at the very heart of his active silence, and of *Bartleby*. What do we mean by this? *Che Vuoi?* is essentially the question asked *to* Bartleby *by* his colleagues time and time again, a question to which he responds with his (articulated, vocalized) active silence. We can almost hear this conversation taking place! Let us imagine for a moment that after much frustration and infuriation, Bartleby's employer asks him, "why are you still here?! You refuse to work so why don't you just simply leave?!" Bartleby responds quietly, "I would prefer not to." His employer offers his exacerbated reply, "Well then! Since you evidently want to stay, tell me what you want from me!!".

"I would prefer not to."

Such a move further hystericizes the narrator, his employer, who simply doesn't seem to enjoy silence in the same way Bartleby does. And it is evident that Bartleby is not enjoying the chatter of his colleagues. Here Lacan's insistence on the analyst's silence is pertinent: a response to the Other's non-response is a key moment in the genesis of the subject. The analyst's silence in the clinic is intended to be provocative, to stimulate discourse, and arguably Bartleby's silence is intended to bring about the opposite—he simply wants to be left alone. However, what happens is that due to his silence his colleagues simply can't stop speaking—to him, and to each other about the matter of Bartleby's silence. In this way, Bartleby functions as an unwitting analyst. The presence of his silence triggers an effect, a rupture in the routine of office discourse. It hystericizes. The effect of silence here is to produce a more urgent speaking around him: this is exactly the trap Bartleby's colleagues fall into. They tried ignoring him, mocking him, kindly engaging him, demanding things of him...Bartleby simply continues to meet his colleague's hysterical speech with his active silence; if he does reply it is reluctantly and repetitiously, "I would prefer not to". This is the source of the fascination Bartleby creates around him (it is as if he makes himself into an agalma, the object-cause of desire).

This also makes the novella's ending ambivalent and arguably failed. The revelation that Bartleby worked in the Dead Letter Office is a desperate and unsatisfying attempt by his colleagues to solve the problem of *Che Vuoi?*—a question that in the end can only be met with silence. The dead letter is the letter that never arrives, is never read and thus has to be destroyed. This was Bartleby's task; to destroy all the letters that will never reach their final destination. The Dead Letter Office can be understood as epitomizing Bartleby's first silent object, where his anguished submission to and repetition of silence began. As Melville's final paragraph goes:

> Dead letters! does it not sound like dead men? ... Sometimes from out the folded paper the pale clerk takes a ring:—the finger it was meant for, perhaps, moulders in the grave; a bank note sent in swiftest charity:—he whom it would relieve, nor eats nor hungers any more; pardon for those who died despairing; hope for those who died unhoping; good tidings for those who died stifling by unrelieved calamities. On errands of life, these letters speed to death. Ah, Bartleby! Ah, humanity!

But the fact that Bartleby works in the Dead Letter Office before meeting the narrator does not answer anything. It does not provide a reason for his active silence at all, but instead serves as a too-convenient, pat answer to the unanswerable question of *Che Vuoi?* (Why was Bartleby doing what he was doing? Ah, he was filled with despair after working in the Dead Letter Office! As Lacan used to say when he wanted to mock some kind of vulgar-Freudian, reductionistic interpretation of someone's symptom, *voila pourquoi votre fille est muette...*) The question of *Che*

Vuoi? cannot be answered not because there has been a failure to communicate but because it is essentially unanswerable. What Bartleby in fact does is embark on creating *ex nihilo*: he actively replaces one melancholic repetition of silence (destroying the letter which does not arrive at its destination) with another (active refusal to work as a scrivener copying legal documents), leaving the question of *Che Vuoi?* directly open via the repetition of his catchphrase. *Che Vuoi?* is far from resolved by Bartleby's active silence.

At the same time Bartleby did not set out to be the Other for his colleagues, however his active silence situates him as precisely this. On the face of it, it seems as though Bartleby *wants* nothing and it is this lack of *wanting* anything or anyone that is inconceivable to those around him. But this is not so clear. Rather, we could say that his desire is a pure desire in that it is a specific desire for nothing whatsoever, nothing in particular. And is this not how the analytic procedure functions; that one (the analysand) is constantly facing the repetition of the analyst's silence as a desire to elicit a speech-act in order to hystericize the symptom? Of course, not being contained in the clinical setting, Bartleby's colleagues experience his silence as a constant frustration—they simply don't know what to do with his mantra. At the same time Bartleby suffers from—enjoys!—his desire for nothing, while his colleagues suffer from being confronted with the enigmatic *jouissance* of his repetitive refusals. The reasons for his negations are inscrutable to those around him. His employer attempts to understand what led to this symptom to no avail. For his employer, Bartleby's silence is hopelessly anti-communal, hence the employer's outcry in the final scene, "Ah Bartleby! Ah humanity!" This outcry, emanating from an anxiety, is a response to how he has interpreted Bartleby's despair generating from previously working at the Dead Letter Office. It seems to help his employer settle the anguish of Bartleby's slow demise. Or we can say—and this is what we contend—that this outcry from his employer marks the point at which he realizes the Other's essential non-response, just when a response was most needed.

It is here that we can think about writing silence and writing unsayability. Paul Valéry's notable, long 'great silence', is a period of his life that followed the death of his mentor Mallarmé. Such was his grief and existential crisis that Valéry did not write for nearly twenty years, ending the period only with the publication of *La Jeune Parque* in 1917. This abandonment of the written word was a commemorative silence. As we have noted Melville also needed space after writing *Moby-Dick*. However, there are other kinds of attempts at writing silence apart from ceasing to write at all. It is at this point that we want to consider Beckett as a writer who attempts to echo literary silences. Importantly, his use of literary silence is unique and is not commemorative, it does not emanate from mourning, nor does it point towards something universal, but rather, is a way to think about the limits of language and its possible effects. Although Beckett certainly grapples with silence, we argue that Beckett provides a good example of what we have in mind with unsayability.

In *Waiting for Godot* (1954 [1982]) there are long moments of inaction and silence, and they emphasize the passing of time in boredom and unease at the growing sense that Godot will not be arriving. These moments preclude any sense of any ultimate, attainable beyond, or that eventually any magnificent insight will be revealed. Although Beckett himself wrote that "every word is like an unnecessary stain on silence and nothingness"[2] his characters often say nothing not because silence must be revered, or out of principle, but more out of simple exhaustion… there is nothing more to say. And, conversely, when they do kill time with their incessant and absurd chatter (wanking around with words) we get the impression that they may as well be silent. Initially, we can place this kind of silence on the side of an active, speaking, linguistically articulated silence. But it is different from that of Bartleby. Beckett shows us how there is a silence that haunts language and does not lie on the other side of it, promising some full meaning. Rather, silence is integral

[2] It is interesting to note that Bartleby's silence differs from Valéry's because it is articulated, repetitively. Furthermore, as we have pointed out, 'I would prefer not to' points towards at least the possibility of future activities and conversations, although we know these won't be undertaken. This mantra, this automated expression of silence, attempts to retrieve something that is disavowed from language. However, it is precisely in the utterances of his mantra that we are prepared for Bartleby's active silence and its unwitting command to his colleagues being retroactively inscribed into linguistic communication. The absence of and struggle to speak directly confront us with the limits of language. For Bartleby, unsayabililty is a technical mishap or glitch in the ontological catastrophe of language. Arguably, both silence and unsayability lead to his classic melancholic response, repeating the mantra that has become the object of his libidinal investment, one which embodies and mediates *unbehagen* as a struggle insisting on the singularity of unsayability. This is the kernel of Melville's novella: although silence is a necessary part of language, the inevitable result of Bartleby's adoption of it is his melancholic position, in which his lost object is ultimately himself.

to the unease and doubt implicit in itself. For Beckett, a relationship to language is all the author ever has and yet it is a tool that will never be mastered. That is not to say that Beckett did not struggle with writing, it is simply that when he did write, what he produced strikes us with its ease and fluidity. And at the end of the day and through his characters, Beckett not only wants to speak but wants his voice heard.

As we have mentioned Beckett's plays are notorious for their long pauses, during which silence and sometimes pantomime take over the stage. This self-effacing, minimalist style that Beckett calls subtractive (in contrast to the densely layered additive style of Joyce) includes texts that appear to mean almost nothing. Perhaps in this way Beckett is deliberately placing himself on the other-side of Joyce. However, many commentators note that what appears to be idle chatter in Beckett's work in fact brilliantly transports us into the worlds of silence, speech, and the experience of unsayability.

Certainly, Beckett himself wrestled with authorship and his desire to be read: "I do not feel like spending the rest of my life writing books that no one will read. It is not as though I wanted to write them" (in Fehsenfeld and Overbeck 2009, p. 209). His fraught relationship to writing, including his position as an author, as we have already noted, is well documented. There were many periods during which he did not write at all for which he gave various reasons without indicating how he ever broke his silences. However, his dedication to language is abundant in his literary texts, and it even shows when he addresses silence.

In his short story, *The Calmative* (1946 [1995]) Beckett explores silence as a connection with a conscious break from the social. The story is part of a trilogy dealing with the subjective experience of forced alienation—old men find themselves destitute, socially side-lined and even expelled from various aspects of social life. Moreover, they actively seem to seek out the alienation they inevitably encounter. *The Calmative* is set during post-war France where terror, anxiety and uncertainty all frame the experience of one man simply referred to as Sam. Sam is a tramp in hiding, not from anyone in particular, but from himself it seems. He is constantly on the move, although he really has no destination in mind. For him, everything that once seemed familiar—his surrounds and people he knows or once knew—is suddenly alien and strange. As readers there are moments where we do question Sam's sanity but in doing so only find ourselves in the realm of Sam's sublime inner-world as we come to realize that is the outside world which is fundamentally lacking. Sam is a vagrant who is well-read in Kant, Shelley, Keats, the Bible and so on. He employs his literary and philosophical insights to cultivate a rich inner monologue which is shared with the reader. The novella itself is the second part of a set of narratives which Beckett refers to as "stories and texts for nothing". The anonymous, passive and frightened Sam in *The Calmative* poignantly says: "All I say cancels out, I'll have said nothing". Beckett continues his literary project on the voice by chronicling a disordered man trying to cope in a disordered world: as Sam says to us in the opening sentence, "I don't know when I died". As he wanders the streets talking to no one, his loss of social identity becomes more profound and despairing. As a response to his terror (not of necessarily of dying as after all, Sam seems to 'return' from the dead in that he continues to live in despair) Sam decides to simply stop speaking. He chooses to offer no account of himself to those who ask and he has no words to offer anyone. He is for the most part silent with others and tends not answer any questions directed at him. He is reduced (and reduces himself) to an invisible vagrant living on the streets and for a time in a forest (where he goes into hiding). He suffers from what we call speech paralysis: he feels compelled to talk at times but simply cannot find the words. He is held hostage by words which cannot be marshalled because language itself is resistant to any effort he undertakes in order to speak. In the end he gives up trying to speak and all we have is his inner monologue as he walks the city alone, terrified to keep living.

Remember that Sam said of himself, "All I say cancels out, I'll have said nothing." What does it mean for language to cancel itself out? Although Sam comes to accept this, even embrace this, it seems that Sam thinks his voice has simply *vanished*. He is rarely listened to and on the odd occasion when he does speak and he gets to a point where he can't be bothered to listen to either himself or anyone else any longer. It is almost as though he accepts that his own voice is his greatest failure. However, it would be a mistake to assume that Sam's terror at an on-going existence is akin to his claim that all he says is nevertheless cancelled out—he doesn't think that he may as well stay silent because no one bothers to listen to him. Rather, it is the opposite: his 'cancelling out' is neither a pathologizing statement nor a complaint. It is for the most part a claim of the passive acceptance with the struggle with words. Beckett's Sam offers the figure of the anonymous, vulnerable and socially insignificant vagrant man as purely inhabiting the position of the barred subject, so much so that the struggle is completely oriented inwards.

Sam is a walker of the city who in refusing the social bond, rejecting the world in which he lingers, cancels out both this world and himself. The only way he can do this is via language. By remaining silent, Sam does not refuse language. This is impossible. And it is not that he is unable to interact with people, occasionally even antagonistically so. Rather, by having fully assumed his barred status he finds himself profoundly *speechless*: for example, when trying to talk to a poor young boy:

> I resolved to speak to him so I marshalled the words and opened my mouth, thinking I would hear them. But all I heard was a kind of rattle, unintelligible even to me who knew what was intended. But it was nothing, mere speechlessness due to long silence, as in the wood that darkens the mouth of hell, do you remember, I only just. (1946 [1995], p. 562)

What is interesting about Sam is not only his frustration, anxiety and shame but also the stain, perhaps upon the word, that his silence brings. Sam's inability to be outwardly eloquent or to even vocally articulate anything at all is embarrassing for him—and one of the very few times it happens in the story. This passage is both heartbreaking and pathetic: the incapacity of the man face-to-face with a small boy. But what it also reveals is that we are inescapably bound to language regardless of whether we speak or not. As we have said, Sam's poignant struggle with language and with remaining silent is starkly revealed in the form of an inner monologue. Sam chooses not to speak because he is frustrated, tired and scared. But it is also true that he simply can't find the words. We are here reminded of Kafka's *A Hunger Artist* (1922) who refused to eat not for deep mystical reason but rather because he simply did not find anything he much liked. The object itself, whether it be the voice or food, is an insubstantial and unsatisfying referent.

There is an inevitable subjective alienation and frustration one is confronted with during unsayability. This is a way in which we can make sense of unsayability, which is arguably the lynchpin of Beckett's way into language. It seems that for Beckett unsayability is located within the order of the social bond—we simply need to struggle with speaking to each other. That is, unsayability is a wrestling with speech precisely because we are inevitably trapped within language. We are subjects of discourse of language and it is this discourse which entraps us. Such entrapment enables a self-conscious voice to emerge (after all, Sam is speaking to himself and to us; ironically we become 'the anonymous') while at the same time rendering the voice as a vanishing object: Sam can't speak to a young child although clearly wanting to, he can't (and sometimes won't) respond to other subjects, he is apprehended by the inability to speak and paralyzed not only by his own voice but the realization that he possesses one which he simply can't use. Sam's vanishing voice which can be thought of as the plausibility of unsayability is an effect of the subject always already being fully interpellated within language.

Many of Beckett's characters are passive, anonymous, even ultimately vagrant, but there is ultimately a significant difference between their respective near silences and that of Melville's Bartleby. Bartleby's silence is a failed attempt to find a way out of language, enabling him to *feel* free, as in some slight momentary release from the hold of language, through repeating 'I would prefer not to'. (Obviously we don't as readers receive the benefit of Bartleby's inner monologue, unlike Beckett's Sam.) Many of Beckett's characters, including Sam as well as Didi and Gogo (from *Godot*) however, are coming from another direction as it were. Inhabiting language in an off-kilter way, they provide a way into language by continuously attempting its traversal, rather than refusing it. The position Beckett's characters are in can be taken as a response to Žižek's challenge that "we feel free because we lack the very language to articulate our unfreedom" (2002, p. 2). Their struggles with language are in fact an effort to articulate their unfreedom, an unfreedom not necessarily emanating from the social bond but due simply to the fact that we are speaking beings inscribed into language, that we are held hostage by language itself. Neither a mystical embrace of silence nor an excess of verbiage can extricate us from the unfreedom associated with language.

Yet on the face of it, what Beckett's characters do is quite close to what apophatic discourse advocates: a practice and an ethic according to which language is at its best when it cancels itself out. In some ways Beckett's Sam reminds us of this position especially. Sometimes it does seem as if Beckett is writing, and his characters are speaking, in order to efface writing and speaking altogether: Sam's "all I say cancels out, I'll have said nothing." But what we want to emphasize, in contrast to what apophatic discourse upholds, is that Beckett's characters situate themselves on the side of the half-saying of truth, Lacan's *mi-dire de la verite*: where there is a struggle with language because everything is only, and can only ever be, half-said. Sam's experience with the unsayable is not a complete divergence away from language entirely (although he does sometimes prefer to remain quiet). Rather, his experience with unsayability entails an encounter with the lack in his ability to vocalise; that speaking words inevitably results simply in nothing, effects nothing; for the most part they are insufficient, useless, ineffectual and pointless. And yet at the same time, speaking needs to be undertaken: it is its lack that drives speaking. At the end of the day Beckett reminds us that with lack (and because of lack) one can still write words or speak (even if, or especially if, they are failed words and of speech itself) and that what cannot be said can still be (partially) written and said.

The will to be silent is not, as we might think, a way to erase the subject and all traces of its existence, but rather a way in which to temporarily disassociate with wrestling with language, as impossible as this is. As already noted, mystical silence takes on the qualities of an object that is supposed to heal the subject's split, or somehow recover something that is lost is speech. Here is the false promise of silence: the closer one gets to it, the less one wrestles with language. However, as we have come to realise, this is simply not the case. We are after all speaking beings structured by language; our *jouissance* lies in the struggle to speak, not in remaining silent. The word ultimately wins out and as Beckett says in *Molloy*, "I am speechless. Followed by speech" (1959, p. 309).

Let us now turn our attention to Cage's famous silent composition, *4′33″* as one that has been claimed by the apophatic tradition. Strictly speaking, *4′33″* is a series of silences; it consists of three movements lasting 33″, 2′40″ and 1′20″, respectively. These silences are performed against the background of the inescapable sounds that occur during the performance of the piece in the concert hall and beyond. However, and to be clear, just sitting in one's office or on the toilet for the same duration is not equal to an experience of *4′33″*. This requires some of the traditional social apparatuses associated with musical performances: an ensemble with its conductor, and of course the presence of an audience in a concert hall or performance space. Sometimes *4′33″* is a solo performance, but usually one piece among others performed at an event. As we are going to argue, a properly staged performance of *4′33″* is more about the spontaneous and incidental sounds emerging during the performance than it is about an impossible quest for silence: or, *4′33″* is about the impossibility of silence. To this extent *4′33″* is a deconstruction of the concept of silence. Silence is promised, expected… and it fails to occur. Cage demonstrates not only that silence is an impossibility but also that it only acquires much of mystique thanks to the presence of sounds.

Although *4′33″* does not minimalize music, the composer, or the performer (after all, the published score includes clear directions for the musicians) there are no specific conduits apart from silence through which *4′33″* speaks. Each space between the movements (that is, the 'non-event' between them in which the audience is permitted to shuffle and cough but not applaud), is determined by using a stop-watch, and the beginning and end of each movement is signalled by the pianist lowering and then raising the lid of the piano. This doesn't not signify any nuanced compositional movement apart from the passing of time, which is composition's most perfunctory task.

There is one performance direction in an earlier arrangement of *4′33″*: the word *tacet* meaning 'to be silent' is given at the beginning of every movement. Interestingly, Cage himself did not give this direction in his original score. He simply wrote that it could be performed by "any instrument or combination of instruments".[3] We want to treat *4′33″* as yet another example of a pragmatics of silence, one that merges with experimental composition, a convergence Cage himself expresses very well when he says about the piece "I have nothing to say and I am saying it" (*Lecture on Nothing*, 1952). Rather than remaining completely silent, *4′33″* articulates silence as a way into the language of music composition and performance. *4′33″* is simply about listening for the silence that passes through noise. For Cage this composition is a movement *into* the impossibility of silence. It seems as if Cage gets the point of language as our hostage-holder: while we fall in love with language, even it if is the language of music, it will never love us back.

In an interview, Cage explained how he was inspired to create *4′33″*. He wanted to experience total silence and so in 1952 entered an anechoic chamber at Harvard University. Instead of silence he heard his blood flowing and what an engineer described as the workings of his nervous system. *4′33″* was created shortly after this encounter with the impossibility of absolute silence (Gann 2010). Realizing this impossibility taught Cage that there is much to hear in silence, that silence is not a beyond, on the other side of language and phenomena.

Cage is also suggesting that musical genres (in this case, Western classical art music) can be problematic when they invoke rules determining what is sonically acceptable and unacceptable. Rather, for Cage, the

[3] The inclusion of the word *tacet* is not unusual in traditional or contemporary composition. It signals that that the musician does not play for an entire section or movement.

function of music is indeterminate insofar as it can draw on a limitless sonic palate. The logical conclusion for Cage is his seminal idea of silence as a procedure, a pragmatics where, although no expressive insight can be found in silence itself, the practice of silence is centred on having nothing to say and leaving the world of sound to chance by simply staying quiet.

Sound is continually taking place and for Cage the experience of every sound is also one of silence which occurs during a specific time-frame (4 minutes and 33 seconds). This Cagean silence emerges through our need for musical self-affirmation, that is, everyone has the ability to develop musical sensibilities in the context of sound rather than on a pure focus on traditional Western art notated composition. Indeed, the highest purpose of art for Cage is simply to have nothing to say. This is for Cage a Zen oriented disposition which is the beginning of art; its very purpose is to say nothing. He offers a comic example of this when insisting that sometimes the most interesting part of listening to a live symphony performance is when the orchestra spend the first ten minutes simply tuning up. Of course, the function of tuning up is purely technical—the cacophony of sounds are nearly always out of time and sometimes out of tune. It can be considered blah blah of the performance to come. However, the strange irony of this is expressed by Cage himself in his *Lecture on Nothing* (1952), in which he articulates a position that we think is quite close to the one we were describing in our section on Beckett: "What we require is silence; but what silence requires is that I go on talking" (in Gann 2010, p. 163).

Cage's position is that performance does not signify anything beyond itself. For Cage, music (organised sound) itself has nothing to say and it doesn't think. Sounds simply act; they rise and fall, become longer and shorter, louder and quiet, and so on. Sounds do not 'talk' and for Cage this is also the very essence of silence. Sound communicates nothing and this in itself should satisfy us. A piece like *4′33″* is supposed to attune us to this. Furthermore, the performance of music does not signify anything apart from itself. Jankélévitch offers a similar position on Western art music, which he claims does not in itself propose anything:

> Music is certainly no system of ideas to be developed discursively, no truth that one must advance toward degree by degree, or whose implications must be explained, or whose import extracted, or whose far-reaching consequences must be made explicit. (2003, p. 69)

Might Jankélévitch be suggesting that performers, listeners, appreciators of music (and he himself!) have nothing to say about it? Of course not! It seems as though we have plenty to say about music; but this is precisely because of its ineffable nature. Everything we say about music is a good example of *mi-dire*.

Let us consider an example. During a live television broadcast of *4′33″*, the following words appeared on the screen as the pianist prepared to 'perform': "You are invited to turn down the volume of your TV set". Even if intended as ironic humour, this invitation entirely misses the point. The background noise from the broadcast coming from the television would be a legitimate part of the performance. (In fact, we would suggest that turning down the volume on the TV would lead to someone *missing* the performance and the very point of it! The sounds in the concert hall, the sounds during the broadcast, would be suppressed….)

4′33″ oscillates between its movements and the intervening spaces that structure it. The performers, far from doing nothing, undertake what performers traditionally do: they keep track of time and experience every sound as a nuanced part of the composition. While the composition itself relies on the traditions of time and performance context as specific experiences to cultivate musical sensibility, the difference in *4′33″* is that no sound is more or less desirable than any other. Cage's proposal for a silent composition for the first time combines deliberate silencing with its articulation, a schema in which sound is neither agreeable nor disagreeable.

In an apt phrase, Khan (1999) refers to Cagean silence as the *impossible inaudible*. That is, one cannot hear everything always occurring in *4′33″* all of the time; and in addition, *not* hearing (the inaudible) is rendered impossible too. Where one sits during the performance, who one sits next to, whether one is a performer or positioned in the audience, all contribute to the context of the sounds that it will be possible to hear. After all, one cannot simply hear nothing (as Cage himself discovered in the anechoic chamber). After one of the earlier performances of *4′33″* in New York, audience members were interviewed about their experiences of it afterwards. The feedback ranged from commentary on the sublime nature of the compositional process (one can imagine that Cage would most certainly have been unimpressed with this interpretation!) to 'not really getting it because I couldn't hear properly as the guy next to me was sniffing the whole time, and others around me were coughing, and…'

(which is precisely what *4′33″* is all about: not trying to listen for anything in particular!).[4] The point of Cage's silent composition is that there is nothing extra or specific to listen for in *4′33″*, that there is nothing sublime to search for. This is very the crux of Cage's silence: beyond the silence every sound is already there, although it is not possible for every sound to be audible all of the time. Cage's silent composition is very much about the eagerness to listen in a particular way; that is, to listen for silence. Yet here sounds are the very condition for this.

We think that Cage poses a specific question: *what makes music, music?* by suggesting that the impossibility of absolute silence plays a part… The bottom line is that to perform *4′33″*, one does not need to know anything specific about music, musicianship or music composition. Yet it is a composed music performance. It could be said that the composition *4′33″* has already 'fallen apart' before it ever begins. This is because *4′33″* explores the everyday contingencies of life, so much so that the composition itself almost becomes an absurdity. One does not need to necessarily possess any talent or skills to even appreciate *4′33″* but rather one simply needs to be prepared to listen, sometimes to the banality of silence. In this context, four minutes and thirty-three seconds may feel like a very long time.

Although it can be said to fall into the realm of absurdity, *4′33″* also signals a theoretical possibility of silence in which pure feeling is attained through listening. The communal intimacy and embodied experience of *4′33″* stays with a person long after the performance has ended. One talks about the *experience* of listening to *4′33″*, not of the rising and falling of the various sounds which make up the compositional elements. We think about the performance and the feelings which may have resonated in the awkward quietness: the annoyance at the passing cars outside, the embarrassment of listening to someone blow their nose, the peculiarity of seeing the seated musicians who are not playing their instruments, all the while abandoning ourselves simply to the passing of time. Simply put, one cannot experience *4′33″* without referring to the

[4]Another amusing anecdote regarding Cage's *4′33″* comes from a personal conversation with Mladen Dolar where he recounts reading a book upon which the male protagonist falls in love with a female classical musician. Knowing nothing about music, but wanting to impress her, he records on cassette tape seven version of *4′33″*, all different, as a gift to her. An apt metaphor for the silence of love!

inward experience of it. It relies on timed pure feeling and nothing more as a compositional form.

However, while 'absence' in *4′33″* is made up of the incidental sounds made by a range of anonymous individuals, this composition is about absolutely nothing in particular. Rather, what is taking place is the willingness to surrender to a context of communal listening. For Cage, this experience lies in the nuanced and precarious relation of sound to silence as an expression within limits, these being the upholding the conventions of context and time. The musicians performing *4′33″* are always prepared. To simply do nothing. They tune their instruments beforehand and are presently silent for entire the performance duration. During this time sound will occur but not from musicians playing their instruments. A different rationality of sound emerges, one in which the musicians are simply unmoving. Silence here can be thought of as *taceo*. The musicians and listeners are prepared for nothing in particular and in such preparedness a traditional character of musical performance, the keeping of time as a compositional foundation, is preserved.

The effect of this nuanced privileging the traditional character of music performance, Cage allows incidental sounds to play out in an aesthetic embracing the impossibility of pure silence. *4′33″* as a composition is dialectical in intent, it is designed to always segue-way into something else: there is no reliability or predictability, but rather it is an incomplete composition of sound which punctuates silence 'right now'. The succession of 'nows' (immediate and unintentional sound) lies not in what is predictable or what it is already written, but in an eruption of opaque and indeterminate 'nows' which may nevertheless be surprising, interesting, mundane, even amusing. Although the composition in which they manifest is of specific duration, any one 'now' is not timed; these 'nows' of everyday life appear uncomposed, not necessarily contrasting with one another and probably not even really connected.

Cagean silence troubles the composition, performance and appreciation of traditional music by exploiting the very sensibilities which have naturalized it. The first note both never arrives and already has. For Cage, sound and silence have a necessary sociality—every sound is potentially music and music as such does not have to actually take place for it to exist. This is pure feeling at its purist: the recognition of music via the negation of the subject together the realisation that the subject itself belongs to only time and the sounds within it. The subject is necessarily in time as an endless series of Cagean 'nows'. Here we might ask the questions how Cage offers a re-re-configuration of silence? The succession of 'nows' for Cage is not in what is already written (that is, composed) but in something more uncertain; the 'nows' that arise during the performance of *4'33"* are spontaneous but they are deliberately uncomposed 'nows'. They are not deliberately contrasted with other 'nows' and probably not even connected to each other (or they are only formally minimally so). What is familiar in *4'33"* are both the command (and impossibility) of silence and the myriad of incidental sounds, but what is not familiar is that this is called 'music', occupying a gap between compositional enunciation and the subject who is the listener, performer, appreciator.... The Cagean silence is a procedure which confirms one thing: despite our desire, absolute and intended silence is impossible.

Despite this impossibility, we can think of silence as force of prohibition. In Munch's *Scream*, Žižek (1996) offers an interesting comment on silence: the scream is certainly silent but this is an unintended silence rather than an absolute, impossible one. The voice represents a powerful, silent object which is nevertheless potentially audible. Žižek describes Munch's *Scream* as silence we "hear with our eyes" (ibid., p. 94). This ratifies an hysteric position in which the imaginary mediator of sound stands in for silence. It is also a position from which the viewer can testify to being a subject.

Hegel mentions an ancient Egyptian sacred statue which, at every sunset, miraculously issues a deep, reverberating sound. Such a mysterious sound magically resonating from within an inanimate object can be seen as a metaphor for the birth of subjectivity. However, at the moment when Munch's Scream resounds we must be careful not to miss the antagonism between a silent scream and a deafening one:

> The true object voice is mute, "stuck in the throat", and what effectively reverberates is the void: resonance always takes place in a vacuum – the tone as such is originally a lament for the lost object [...] In this precise sense, as Lacan points out, voice and silence relate as figure and ground: silence is not (as one would be prone to think) the ground against which the figure of the voice emerges; quite the contrary, the reverberating sound itself provides the ground that renders visible the figures of silence [...]. In other words, their relationship is mediated by an impossibility: ultimately, we hear things because we cannot see. everything. (Žižek 1996, p. 93)

We think that Bartleby's active silence confronts us with a radical form of desire, perhaps even of pure desire. Žižek correctly associates this radical form of desire with the "formal gesture of refusal as such... strictly analogous to Sygne's *No!*" (2006, pp. 384–385). Lacan makes a decisive statement regarding the debt to language in Sygne's *No!* as well as in Claudel's plays in Seminar VIII:

> To us, the Word is not simply the law into which we insert ourselves in order that each of us bear responsibility for the debt that constitutes our fate. It opens up for us the possibility or temptation on the basis of which it is possible for us to curse ourselves, not only as a particular destiny or life, but as the very pathway by which the Word commits us, and as an encounter with the truth, as the moment of truth. We are no longer solely subject to feeling guilty owing to symbolic debt. We can, in the most proximate sense that the word indicates, be reproached for bearing responsibility for the debt. In short, it is the very debt that gave us our place that can be stolen from us; and it is in this context that we can feel totally alienated from ourselves. Antiquity's *Até* no doubt made us guilty of this debt, but to give it up – as we can now – makes us responsible for a still greater misfortune owing to the fact that fate is no longer anything [for us]. (1960–1961 [2015], p. 302)

No! can be uttered in many ways and not always by using the word. Here, Lacan's meditation on Sygne's No! gives us insight into his approach to enunciation and our indebtedness to language. Unlike Bartleby, Sygne de Coûfontaine, the protagonist in Claudel's *The Hostage* (1917 [2009]), is explicit about her refusal, or rather inability, to utter the word, *No!*. Her *No!* is the most explicit when, before dying from a bullet wound, she is visited by a priest (in one of the two endings Claudel proposes) who offers her comfort and absolution. Her emphatic refusal, *No!* represents a radical loss of self and this is arguably her ultimate sacrifice as well as her freedom. While Sygne compulsively shakes her head no, she enacts *No!* without ever uttering it. It is a bodily utterance. Why is the authority of *No!* so lost on her? We will get to this in a minute, but first, in Seminar VIII Lacan notes the strange ambiguity of her name:

> There is, moreover an imperceptible change, the substitution of the y for the I, where one can recognize in this superimposition of the mark... [an] imposition of the signifier upon [the subject which] is at the same time that which marks and disfigures... [Sygne]. (1960–1961 [2015], p. 352)

Her name is uncanny; she bodily becomes her name as a performative signifier of the Symbolic Order, as Župančič puts it, "Sygne makes a sign of no" (2000, p. 228). During the French Revolution, while hiding the Pope whom her cousin George had released from captivity, the Revolutionary guards enter the House of Coûfontaine, confronting her with the ultimate false choice. Their leader, the executioner Turelure, offers Sygne an ultimatum: marry him, thereby making him the next Lord of Coûfontaine, or be arrested and have all her worldly possessions and estate confiscated. She appears to sacrifice her desire in the effort to retain her family sovereignty by marrying Turelure, and eventually they have a son. This is a sacrifice she takes part into preserve her desire to continue her family legacy in the face of failed authority. However, she is not going to let him have everything her family have worked for; being her heir her son will become her first unspoken *No!* to Turelure. During the course of her marriage Sygne develops the nervous habit of shaking her head left and right, without ever uttering the word itself. Here Claudel's stage directions are explicit: "Throughout the [third] act Sygne has a nervous twitching of the head from side to side, as though saying 'No'" (1917 [2009], p. 63). It is when Sygne attempts suicide by intercepting the bullet meant for her loathed husband (fired by her beloved cousin George) that she delivers her second and more significant *No!* to Turelure. He begs to know why she did this: was it out of love for him or a desire for salvation? He desperately implores her forgiveness but she refuses to speak, only shaking her head and grimacing as she dies (in the second ending Claudel wrote for the play). She is, as Lacan states in *Écrits*, the hostage of the word with her grimace standing in for an absent speech (1966 [2002]). Her self-sacrifice, that is, her marriage to Turelure, culminates in her refusal to speak in the name of a wider ideological cause and or her perceived honour in dying all provide Sygne's reason for living, thereby supporting both her Symbolic Order and her ultimate anxiety, an anxiety which manifests as a response to failed authority. She cannot utter the crucial word because she has had to replace her desire (for sovereignty) with other less desirable objects; the most obvious being that she marries a man she despises and has a son with him, despite her true desire to be with her cousin, George. Sygne is the placeholder for the word itself: *No!*. And it is the word that is the silent drive which paves Sygne's destiny. It is one thing to know what one wants and quite another to articulate it. In her abandonment of the word Sygne simultaneously locates herself as a prisoner of it. Utterance of the word *No!* is in itself inadequate; Sygne identifies with the word and symbolises herself within it as an object. The word for Sygne becomes not only the law but the unsayability to come precisely because she accepts her destiny. This is the reduction of the word, in this case the utterable word, to the law of language. Lacan makes a poignant statement in his reading of Claudel's Sygne: "man becomes a hostage of the Word because he tells himself...that God is dead" (1960–1961 [2015], p. 354). Sygne is unable to say *No!* because she has had to be complicit to the unsayability of her circumstances. So she is forced to half-say yes, while her body half-speaks, *No!*

Such *mi-dire* is the style and condition of unsayability of the structure and nature of language itself. That is, that which is partially expressed bonds the subject to also what is absent in speech. We could say that that which is not enunciated, which does not 'arrive' as such, or lacks a destination, leaves open the possibility that more can potentially be said at some other time and in another context. But this would locate language as some false ideal. Rather, what is half-said is a way of contending with the potency of what actually is said. Here we can speculate that what is not said is a way of wrestling with the very limits of language and a product of meaning-effects; and not necessarily a will to remain silent.

References

Beckett, S. (1946 [1995]). The Calmative. In *The Complete Short Prose, 1929–1989*. New York: Grove Press.

Beckett, S. (1953). *Watt*. Paris: Olympia Press.

Beckett, S. (1954 [1982]). *Waiting for Godot: A Tragedy in Two Acts*. New York: Grove Press.

Beckett, S. (1959). *Molloy, Malone Dies, the Unnamable*. London: Calder and Boyars.

Cage, J. (1952). *Silence: Lectures and Writings*. Middletown: Wesleyan University Press.

Claudel, P. (1917 [2009]). *The Hostage: A Drama*. Ithaca: Cornell University Library.

Fehsenfeld, M. D., & Overbeck, L. M. (2009). *Letters of Samuel Beckett 1929–1940*. Cambridge: Cambridge University Press.

Gann, J. (2010). *No Such Thing as Silence: John Cage's 4'33"*. New Haven: Yale University Press.

Jankélévitch, V. (1996). Le Pardonner? *Le Monde*. Paris.

Jankélévitch, V. (2003). *Music and the Ineffable* (C. Abbate, Trans.). Princeton and Oxford: Princeton University Press.
Kafka, F. (1922). A Hunger Artist. *Die neue Rundschau.* Berlin: S. Fischer Verlag.
Khan, D. (1999). *Noise Water Meat: A History of Sound in the Arts.* Cambridge: MIT Press.
Lacan, J. (1960–1961 [2015]). *Seminar VIII: Transference* (B. Fink, Trans.). Cambridge: Polity.
Lacan, J. (1966–1967). *La logique du fantasme.* Unpublished typescript.
Lacan, J. (1966 [2002]). *Écrits* (B. Fink, Trans.). New York: W. W. Norton.
Melville, H. (1853). *Bartleby the Scrivener: A Story of Wall Street.* New York: Putnam.
Nasio, J.-D. (1987). *Le silence en psychanalyse.* Paris: Payot.
Žižek, S. (1996). I Hear You with My Eyes. In S. Žižek & R. Salecl (Eds.), *Gaze and Voice as Love Objects.* Durham: Duke University Press.
Žižek, S. (2002). *Welcome to the Desert of the Real.* London: Verso.
Žižek, S. (2006). *The Parallax View.* Cambridge: MIT Press.
Župančič, A. (2000). *The Ethics of the Real: Kant and Lacan.* London: Verso.

CHAPTER 4

The Silent Treatment

When I consider the short duration of my life,
swallowed up in an eternity before and after,
the little space I fill engulfed in the infinite immensity of spaces
whereof I know nothing,
and which know nothing of me,
I am terrified.
The eternal silence of these infinite spaces frightens me.

Pascal, *Pensées*

Abstract In the final chapter we look at Lacan's provisional uptake of Pascal and elaborate on this as a way of understanding silence as crucial in psychoanalysis and in everyday life. We contend that the impossibility of silence is a quest worth embarking on as it raises a number of questions about subjectivity and its relation to truth.

Keywords Pascal · *Pensées* · Pascal's wager · Libertines · Lacan · Goldmann (Lucien) · Science · Silence · Descartes' cogito

We have spent the last two chapters discussing silence, unsayability and their intrinsic relation to language. Lacanian psychoanalysis presents us with a position that we compared earlier to the Stockholm syndrome: we are held hostage by language, and Lacanian psychoanalysis urges us to fall in love with our hostage taker. Or, to change the metaphor, if we are

E. Pluth and C. Zeiher, *On Silence*, The Palgrave Lacan Series,
https://doi.org/10.1007/978-3-030-28147-2_4

stuck within the cave of language, we are asked to become true and willing captives! This is a difficult position to maintain, especially since when we experience that the love we feel is unreciprocated, we may feel abandoned and betrayed. Here we become aware that the opposite of love is not hate, but despair.[1] Again, according to the table we presented in Chapter 1, Lacanian psychoanalysis presents us with a position in which both language and silence are positively charged:

Language	Silence
+	+

But we are at a point now where we can ask, as one might at the end of an analysis, precisely what is it that we *gain*, if anything, from loving our captor, language? Here again we are forced to contend with not only language's limits but that we can never take the word at its own word, that is we can't take language at face-value. In the previous chapter we noted that while it may be possible, even worthwhile, to become hostages to language, it never does love us back; it never did and it never will. Melville, Beckett and Cage showed us different ways of handling the failure and loss entailed by inevitably becoming speaking-beings. While we want to align their positions with that of Lacanian psychoanalysis, we have to admit that they are also close to another position we alluded to in Chapter 1, in which *both* language and silence are devalued (in contrast to apophatic discourse which, recall, undervalues language while overvaluing silence). We might say that this position entails an identification with language and silence that is charged with despair, making up part of a tragic worldview. We said we would associate this position with Pascal, whose position according to our original matrix is as follows:

Language	Silence
–	–

[1] In another respect, we could say that our hostage-taker up to this point has been Lacan. His orientation has provided a way for us to think about language in all its nuances. We have encountered a few others also, Franke, Jankélévitch and Badiou; far from deterring us from thinking silence, they have enabled us ways into thinking about it as a singular category.

The silence of infinite space frightens him, and language offers no consolation.[2]

About the well-known passage from Pascal serving as exergue to this chapter, Koyré observes (in a footnote in *From the Closed World to the Infinite Universe*) that the one who utters it should not be taken to be Pascal himself, but rather the atheist-libertine figure with whom he is in constant dialogue. Why would it be just such a figure who would feel terror before an empty, a-signifying cosmos? Most of the atheists and libertines we know don't feel anything like this at all (and perhaps even consider the dread laughable). Why is the silence of the cosmos instead not reassuring to Pascal's libertine? Why wouldn't it be taken to indicate the absence of eternal damnation, for example? Or, perhaps this silence and the dread before it are in fact the cause of the libertine's behaviour—the pursuit of pleasure motivated by an attempt to escape from dread? Might this be Pascal's view? Or is that too existentialist?

Consider the difference between Pascal's figure and the contemporary naturalist, who, far from feeling terror at the emptiness of the cosmos, is inclined to experience giddiness and wonder before it. Think of the enthusiasm of specialists and celebrities like Neil de Grasse Tyson, and his pop cultural precursor, Carl Sagan. To them, the universe is filled with wonders and mysteries, billions and billions of them that inspire us to explore, to know…yet we are supposed to remain oblivious or indifferent to nature's infinite emptiness and inhumanity. Werner Herzog's *The Wild Blue Yonder* (2005) seems to be a film that is trying to restore that Pascalian dread. (We could say that *Grizzly Man* is doing the same thing from another perspective.) In an interview, Herzog said that his inspiration for the film came from a fact that science fiction typically overlooks: the amount of time actual interstellar travel would take is such that whatever species departed on such voyages would likely not even be the same as the species that arrived! (In the interim, evolution would have kicked in…). Perhaps one of the ideological services people like Tyson and Sagan perform is that they replace the silence and indifference of the cosmos with a universe that once again speaks and signifies. And

[2] In Seminar VIII, Lacan remarks that the "eternal silence only scares us *a moitié*" and further attributes this to science having "expulsed the subject from language. It creates its formulas with a language voided of the subject, and, Lacan adds, this rejection/throwing of the subject outside of the symbolic and its reappearance in the real have an effect on the history of science. This effect is the new linguistics" (1960–1961 [2015], p. 129).

it gives humanity a purpose—both epistemological and colonial. Instead of pursuing pleasure in all manner of questionable practices, as Pascal's libertine did, this contemporary ideology amounts to taking pleasure in what otherwise should be causing dread and anxiety. Ironically, such promoters of science are actually contributing to the return of a pre-modern condition: the re-enchantment of the universe, which is an enjoyment that not only re-establishes harmony, but inscribes the subject right into its very heart. Let's not forget Kant's famous line about the two things that filled the mind with wonder—the moral law within, and the starry heavens above.

We think we can associate this position with what Lacan described as science's suturing of the subject. What did he mean by this? Lacan linked psychoanalysis to the rise of the modern sciences not in order to argue that it is a natural science, but to point out that it works with a particular subject that emerged along with the scientific worldview. Yet at the same time, at the very moment of this subject's emergence, Lacan claims that science sutured that same subject. At this very juncture psychoanalytic discourse and scientific discourse part ways. Psychoanalysis takes up and deals with the subject otherwise closed off and ignored by the sciences.

The suturing of the subject is something we read as an equation of the individual with the ego, whereas the subject of science, the subject of psychoanalysis (according to Lacan one and the same thing) is the split subject of the unconscious. The idea that science sutures the subject amounts to saying that the natural sciences are not equipped to deal with the unconscious, and with a subject that is nothing but that which is represented by a signifier for another signifier. For whatever reason, when it comes to the subject and the unconscious Lacan thinks the sciences actually regress, promoting a notion of the subject (as ego) that is full, self-present, spherical... In short, the sciences (and philosophy) hang on to the soul: a philosophical, humanist, religious subject. In Lacan's opinion these are all traits that are characteristic not of the modern break but of what preceded it, whatever it is called (Milner calls it the ancient *episteme*).

But we find something different in Pascal. Perhaps Lacan should have said that the subject of psychoanalysis is Pascalian instead of Cartesian. Or at least that Pascal presents us with something like the preconditions for the psychoanalytic subject-position. We think that Pascal defers the suturing of the subject of science/psychoanalysis a bit longer than

Descartes did, and we find this in the dread he describes before the silence of infinite space, as well as in his famous wager. It is well known that Lacan liked to consider different ways in which the Cartesian cogito could be parsed such that it would line up with the subject of psychoanalysis: "I think, 'therefore I am'" being one of his better-known versions of it. Parsing the cogito this way was a way to defer what Lacan considers to be Descartes's own suturing of the subject, in which it became, as quickly as possible, a thinking substance attributed with a number of qualities (doubting, willing, perceiving, refusing, sensing, imagining…). The cogito that lines up with the Lacanian split subject is one that is radically reduced, we could say. As Milner reads it, it is a mathematized thought, a thought stripped bare of its qualities, in a gesture that is continuous with the Galilean mathematization and quantification of the natural world. In this respect, Lacan saw psychoanalysis as a further step forward in the Galilean project, a mathematizing of the subject itself.

We think Lucien Goldmann captures this point well in his book on Pascal, even if his own notion of the subject is still too existentialist and humanist. Goldmann suggests that Pascal is the first truly dialectical thinker: "For Pascal himself, there is really only one position which he regards as valid: that of the tragic dialectic which replies both 'Yes' and 'No' to all the fundamental problems created by man's life and by his relationship with the universe and his fellows" (1964 [2016], p. 11). Elaborating on what he calls the tragic worldview, developed to its fullest in his *Pensées*, Goldmann writes:

> The nature of the tragic mind in seventeenth-century France can be characterized by two factors: the complete and exact understanding of the new world created by rationalistic individualism, together with all the invaluable and scientifically valid acquisitions which this offered to the human intellect; and, at the same time, the complete refusal to accept this world as the only one in which man could live, move, and have his being. (ibid., p. 35)

The division Goldmann points to here is one between the increasing confidence in our know-how with the universe thanks to quantification and mathematization, and an increasing discomfort with the silence and inhumanity of that very universe (the cosmos, the gods, no longer speak, and also no longer mean anything; nature is reduced to quantities, qualities are removed from it). This is Pascal's unique dialectical position according to Goldmann, the "yes" and "no" that his subject position straddles.[3]

Consider the feeling after one of those planetarium shows at a natural history museum. You get barraged with outstanding visuals about the scale of the solar system, the galaxy, the universe, the vast amounts of time and space separating us from our planetary and celestial neighbours and origins... you're basically pummelled with how insignificant and futile we are, you become increasingly sure of humanity's demise and futility...nothing one does *really* matters... and at the end of it you're expected to feel awe and wonder at your own insignificance—after all, no one is really special, we are all equally shitty. And to add insult to injury, at the end you're typically asked to make a financial contribution for more research into this melancholic portrayal of nothingness (as if knowledge is going to save us from anything...)! Really, there should be suicide counsellors on staff at these places. Imagine how some of our favourite thinkers would respond to such a visit on a sunny Saturday afternoon: somehow it would make Kant feel morally superior to everything, Hegel may try not to show any concern ("*So ist es...*"), Lacan, like Hegel, might be a little nonchalant but would maybe string some knots together, figuring out a topology to capture the terror of nothingness...but what would Pascal be doing? Would he be curled up in a foetal position, terrified at the horror of it all? Or, like his libertine, would he resolve to dedicate his life to the pursuit of pleasure? Or, of course in a third option, would he feel the urge to gamble on the existence of God and immortality, convincing himself that this is the only real choice?

The position we're describing here also makes us think of Alvie Singer, the protagonist in Woody Allen's *Annie Hall*, who as a young boy became depressed when he found out that the universe was

[3]A provocative thesis, in light of which it is interesting to note that Pascal appears briefly on only one page in Hegel's entire *History of Philosophy*, and that is in the introduction—it is a passing reference in which Hegel expresses some praise for the "brightest gleams of thought" in the *Pensées*. Despite this, Pascal apparently was not worthy of his own entry in the rest of the history, and Hegel seems to have found Pascal to be merely an edifying religious thinker (Hegel, I, p. 93). This is quite underwhelming given that Pascal and Hegel seemed to perhaps share a philosophical comradery: when push came to shove, they were both willing to stand within a possible dread as a certainty, against any kind of falsity. In this way, they both tarry with hesitating, doubt, and anxiety as essential parts of the procedure of thinking.

expanding. (Maybe he had just been visiting one of those planetarium shows…). His mother's rebuttal is worth repeating: "what is that your problem? You live in Brooklyn! Brooklyn's not expanding!"

Alvie's mother was not about to let her son fall from Jewish grace into the void of speculative science. As far as she was concerned, the burden of proof lies with science, not faith, and who better than to convince Alvie of the status quo than the exemplary man of science himself: their family doctor, Dr. Flicker. So off they go and pay him a visit to be reassured that the man of science can confirm what the Jewish mother already knew: "Brooklyn won't be expanding for millions of years! And we've got to try and enjoy ourselves while we are here, hey?"

The reaction of Alvie's mother falls somewhere between the dread of Pascal's libertine and the excitement of the contemporary naturalist: *what is there really to be so concerned about in any of this?!* This reaction gives us some comic relief, a diversion from the position of the naturalist's giddiness (which actually seems to have a negative effect on Alvie) and Alvie's own sudden spiral into melancholy. Our dismal anxiety about our mortality literally drives us to distraction and serves as a constant reminder of the terror we are avoiding. Why on earth would one want to contemplate the terrible nothingness before us, when instead we can just distract ourselves with reason or pleasure instead? This is precisely the position of Alvie's mother—unintendedly comic in her hyper-pragmatic labour of love and also in her own effort not to feel trapped within an infinity that cannot be comprehended. Trying to appease her son's anguish (as well as arguably her own), she simply tells him in not so many words to stop talking nonsense. Her wager is that without hesitation one ought to be on the side of 'common sense'—it is abundantly obvious that Brooklyn is not expanding! And if the universe happens to be expanding (we think that this might have touched a nerve…), Alvie still has nothing really to lose, because after all, it doesn't much affect Brooklyn. In this way, Alvie's mothers captures perfectly the finality of Pascal's wager (with the help of a third party, their family doctor who, while enjoying a cigarette, simply agrees with Alvie's mother): contending with one's inability to believe as a reasoned choice. After all, not everything is necessarily uncertain! There is no doubt! Look at Brooklyn, it's not going anywhere!

It's a bit surprising that Lacan would discuss Pascal at all: he seems rather out-of-date and held deep religious convictions. But Lacan was convinced that there is a connection between Pascal's wager and the conditions for psychoanalysis. Lacan had a long-standing interest in Jansenism (and a rather sizable library on it), a movement Pascal was part of (Hoens 2018–2019, p. 97). Lacan was also interested in Pascal the man, who in many ways seemed to live a life devoid of (or avoiding) desire; he was committed to celibacy and was not interested in individuating from his father or his brilliant sister, Jacqueline (who ended up 'escaping' to the convent once their father had died, much to the chagrin of her brother). His very subjectivity and attraction to austerity interested Lacan as much as his contributions to mathematics and thinking did.

The lesson Lacan takes from Pascal's wager is that we can't be inactive or neutral. We can't determine truth via reason alone, so we have to live out life as a wager. That is, because we are captives of the cosmos, so to speak, we have to exist in it, be a part of it. We simply have no choice. For Lacan, how we think ourselves within the infinity of the cosmos is structured by language. For Pascal it was the silent, infinite cosmos that held us captive, yet also could not be all there was—this is his tragic worldview. Hence his wager on the infinite happiness entailed by the existence of God: why not make such a bet? All alternative choices make no sense, and are frankly bad bets given the stakes are understood properly. For Lacan it is language that is the hostage-taker and that acts in the place of the cosmos. And it is this that we must invest in.

Silence confronts the subject not only with its own division, but with its investment in this division. When confronted with the void of language, whether it lead to an inability to speak, or to an anxiety about speaking, the subject faces lack with it. In this way silence can be thought of as the not-all of speaking. Of course, as we seen, silence does not always signify lack: as apophatic discourse shows us, quite the contrary. But Pascal's position is an interesting intermediary between the apophatic tradition and psychoanalysis, in that its centre point is not silence as God, or as contact with the real, but silence as the silence of the Other—exactly what Lacanian psychoanalysis posits as the very *energion* of the subject.

This kind of meaningful silence as a relation to God is noted by Goldmann when quoting Lukacs:

> He [the tragic, modern man] hopes that a judgment by God will illuminate the different struggles which he sees in the world before him and will reveal the ultimate truth. But the world around him still follows the same

> path, indifferent to both questions and answers. No word comes from either created or natural things, and the race is not to the swift nor battle to the strong. The clear voice of the judgment of God no longer sounds out about the march of human destiny, for the voice which once gave life to all has now fallen silent. Man must live alone and by himself? The voice of the Judge has fallen silent forever, and this is why man will always be vanquished, doomed to destruction in victory even more than in defeat. (Goldmann, pp. 35–36, quoting Lukacs, *Die Selle und die Formen*, pp. 332–333)

Again, for Goldmann this is an expression of what he calls Pascal's tragic worldview. Does this not also echo the clinic in some ways? Might Goldmann be unwittingly hinting at the analyst's silence here?

Dolar, when he reflects on silence in his book on the voice, also refers to Pascal, and argues that Pascal's is far from a mystical silence: it is to be associated with the rupture made by modern science. It is the silence of a universe "that has ceased to speak"—one that "is no longer the expression of the supreme sense, of harmony, of God's wise plan" (2006, pp. 155–156). A universe that has "stopped making sense" (ibid., p. 156). But the difference between Pascal and psychoanalysis is found with the silence of the drives, which are not, like Pascal's silence, the silence of a nature, but of a decentred nature, a nature not other to signifiers but affected by them.

In a way we can also say that silence is a glue that holds words together: think of how Lacan says that the Other's desire can be encountered in the gaps between words. This is what we have been calling the symbolic dimension of silence, but it is also where we find an exposure to the real. Does this not turn silence into a signifier? Perhaps to say that silence is a signifier is going too far: silence as the sometimes-imperceptible space between signifiers does not in itself count as one, but has its effects in a sort of chain. This is why silence in the clinic functions less like a signifier than as a form of punctuation (we discussed scanding earlier): its function is to produce an effect within the signifying chain. It does this deliberately (or perhaps, not) through a communicative structure. Silence can insert an intended meaning (pause for effect) or unintended one (stunned silence) to show "the subject that he is saying more than he thinks he is" (1953–1954 [1991], p. 54). Of course, in the clinic this is a deliberate technique, but we can also say that we do this all the time.

When one enters into analysis, the only commitment is to speaking. There really is no right or privilege to remain silent at all for the analysand, although as we have said, silence plays a crucial role. However, one simply cannot attend analytic session after analytic session and not say a thing. Even if silences permeate the analytic sessions, the analysand will eventually need to say something.[4] In the end the realization is that language is all that one has. The position the analyst adopts is one of "the instrument which enables the patient to make a 'full' statement" (Nobus 2000, p. 66). For the analysand, there will come a time when there is simply no choice but to speak.

It is easy to think of psychoanalysis as tragic in its vision of the subject. Lacan himself states that, "[t]here is something originally, inaugurally, profoundly wounded in the human relation to the world" (1933 [1988], p. 167) and that "[l]ife does not want to be healed" (ibid., p. 233). There are a plethora of tragic moments emphasized by Lacanian theory: the mirror stage insists upon the necessity of alienation; the analyst's silence contends directly with the analysand's sense of destitution; the ego is symptomatic of that which cannot be spoken…What we realize by putting silence to work is how it is possible to enjoy our state of non-Being, how it is possible to actively take up an affair with language, our hostage taker.

We think that this affair between language and silence goes a bit further—silence is like the silent partner to language, the hostage taker. The mode of silence highlighted by psychoanalysis is not its otherness to language but its intrinsic relationship to it. Silence is not an other to the Other but rather it is wrapped up with articulation, it itself articulates, and it is both insufficient to and in excess of the logic of language while also being fully inscribed into the logic of language for speaking beings. It is both a rest in the movement of language and, despite its reputation, does not necessarily bear the traits of an absolute otherness, an absolute beyond. And Lacan holds that the psychoanalytic subject is the result of this strange mixture. Silence in its absolute form is impossible and there is nothing self-identical to it: it is a category of its own that allows the word to break into or break out from it. It is here that we encounter silence as the moment which really does get the last word on language.

[4]Even then, there is not 'complete silence'. The analysand hears the analyst breathing, shift around in her chair, the pen scrawling on paper as she takes notes and so on. The thing is that these are not communicative silences or intended to be.

References

Dolar, M. (2006). *The Voice and Nothing More*. Cambridge: MIT Press.

Goldmann, L. (1964 [2016]). *The Hidden God: A Study of Tragic Vision in the Pensées of Pascal and the Tragedies of Racine*. London: Verso.

Herzog, W. (Director). (2005). *The Wild Blue Yonder* [Film]. United Kingdom: Werner Herzog Film Production.

Hoens, D. (2018–2019). *The Logic of Love: A Conceptual Study of Lacan's Formalization of the Subject-Object Relation*. PhD diss., Department of Psychology, Ghent University.

Lacan, J. (1933 [1988]). Motives of Paranoid Crime: The Crime of the Papin Sisters. *Critical Texts, 5*, 7–11.

Lacan, J. (1953–1954 [1991]). *Seminar I: Freud's Papers on Technique* (J.-A. Miller, Ed.). Cambridge: Cambridge University Press.

Lacan, J. (1960–1961 [2015]). *Seminar VIII: Transference* (B. Fink, Trans.). Cambridge: Polity.

Nobus, D. (2000). *Jacques Lacan and the Freudian Practice of Psychoanalysis*. London: Routledge.

References

A Day in the Life of a Trappist Monk. Accessed from virtualmuseum.ca.

Agamben, G. (1998). *Homo Sacer: Sovereign Power and Bare Life*. Palo Alto, CA: Stanford University Press.

Allen, W. (Director). (1977). *Annie Hall* [Film]. United States: United Artists.

Badiou, A. (1992). Conférence sur la soustraction. In *Conditions*. London: Bloomsbury.

Barthes, R. (1977–1978 [2002]). *The Neutral* (R. Krauss & D. Hollier, Trans.). New York: Columbia University Press.

Beckett, S. (1953). *Watt*. Paris: Olympia Press.

Beckett, S. (1959). *Molloy, Malone Dies, the Unnamable*. London: Calder and Boyars.

Beckett, S. (1967). *Eh Joe and Other Writings*. London: Faber and Faber.

Beckett, S. (1946 [1995]). The Calmative. In *The Complete Short Prose, 1929–1989*. New York: Grove Press.

Beckett, S. (1954 [1982]). *Waiting for Godot: A Tragedy in Two Acts*. New York: Grove Press.

Cage, J. (1952). *Silence: Lectures and Writings*. Middletown: Wesleyan University Press.

Claudel, P. (1917 [2009]). *The Hostage: A Drama*. Ithaca: Cornell University Library.

Dinouart, A. (1771). *L'art de se taire, principalement en matière de religion*. Paris: Petite Bibliothèque Payot.

Dolar, M. (2006). *The Voice and Nothing More*. Cambridge: MIT Press.

E. Pluth and C. Zeiher, *On Silence*, The Palgrave Lacan Series,
https://doi.org/10.1007/978-3-030-28147-2

Edwards, R., & Reader, K. (2001). *The Papin Sisters*. Oxford: Oxford University Press.

Fehsenfeld, M. D., & Overbeck, L. M. (2009). *Letters of Samuel Beckett 1929–1940*. Cambridge: Cambridge University Press.

Fink, B. (1997a). *The Lacanian Subject: Between Language and Jouissance*. Princeton: Princeton University Press.

Fink, B. (1997b). *A Clinical Introduction to Lacanian Psychoanalysis Theory and Technique*. Cambridge: Harvard University Press.

Fliess, R. (1949). Silence and Verbalisation: A Supplement to the Theory of the 'Analytic Rule'. *International Journal of Psycho-Analysis 30*, 21–30.

Fontaneau, F. (1999). *L'Ethique du silence. Wittgenstein et Lacan*. Paris: Seuil.

Franke, W. (2007a). *On What Cannot Be Said: Apophatic Discourses in Philosophy, Religion, Literature, and the Arts. Volume 1. Classic Formulations*. Notre Dame, IN: Notre Dame Press.

Franke, W. (2007b). *On What Cannot Be Said: Apophatic Discourses in Philosophy, Religion, Literature, and the Arts. Volume 2. Modern and Contemporary Transformations*. Notre Dame, IN: Notre Dame Press.

Franke, W. (2014). *A Philosophy of the Unsayable*. Notre Dame, IN: Notre Dame Press.

Franzini, A. (1987). Une aphonie éloquente. In Sous la direction de J.-D. Nasio, *Le silence en psychanalyse* (pp. 123–134). Paris: Petite Bibliothèque Payot.

Freud, S. (1912). The Dynamics of Transference. In *The Standard Edition of the Complete Psychological Works of Sigmund Freud*. London: Hogarth.

Freud, S. (1919). The Uncanny. In *The Standard Edition of the Complete Psychological Works of Sigmund Freud*. London: Hogarth.

Freud, S. (1926). Inhibitions, Symptoms and Anxiety. In *The Standard Edition of the Complete Psychological Works of Sigmund Freud*. London: Hogarth.

Gann, J. (2010). *No Such Thing as Silence: John Cage's 4'33"*. New Haven: Yale University Press.

Goldmann, L. (1964 [2016]). *The Hidden God: A Study of Tragic Vision in the Pensées of Pascal and the Tragedies of Racine*. London: Verso.

Grigg, R. (1997). The Concept of Semblant in Lacan's Teaching. *Lacan.com*. Accessed from http://www.lacan.com/griggblog.html.

Hegel, G. W. F. (1892 [1940]). *Einleitung in die Geschichte der Philosophie* (J. Hoffmeister, Ed.). Hamburg: Felix Meiner Verlag.

Herzog, W. (Director). (2005). *The Wild Blue Yonder* [Film]. United Kingdom: Werner Herzog Film Production.

Hoens, D. (2018–2019). *The Logic of Love: A Conceptual Study of Lacan's Formalization of the Subject-Object Relation*. PhD diss., Department of Psychology, Ghent University.

Jankélévitch, V. (1996). Le Pardonner? *Le Monde*. Paris.

Jankélévitch, V. (2003). *Music and the Ineffable* (C. Abbate, Trans.). Princeton and Oxford: Princeton University Press.

Jankélévitch, V., & Hobart, A. (1996). Do Not Listen to What They Say, Look at What They Do. *Critical Inquiry, 22*(3), 549–551. http://www.jstor.org/stable/1344022.

Johnston, A. (2015). This Philosophy Which Is Not One: Jean-Claude Milner, Alain Badiou, and Lacanian Antiphilosophy. *S-Journal, 3*, 137–158.

Kafka, F. (1922). A Hunger Artist. *Die neue Rundschau*. Berlin: S. Fischer Verlag.

Khan, D. (1999). *Noise Water Meat: A History of Sound in the Arts*. Cambridge: MIT Press.

Kojève, A. (1949 [1969]). *Introduction to the Reading of Hegel: Lectures on the Phenomenology of Spirit* (J. Nichols, Trans.). Ithaca: Cornell University Press.

Koyré, A. (1968). *From the Closed World to the Infinite Universe*. Baltimore: John Hopkins University Press.

Lacan, J. (1933 [1988]). Motives of Paranoid Crime: The Crime of The Papin Sisters. *Critical Texts, 5*, 7–11.

Lacan, J. (1953–1954 [1991]). *Seminar I: Freud's Papers on Technique* (J.-A. Miller, Ed.). Cambridge: Cambridge University Press.

Lacan, J. (1956–1957 [1994]). *Livre IV: La relation d'objet et les structures freudiennes* (J.-A. Miller, Ed.). Paris: Seuil.

Lacan, J. (1957–1958 [2017]). *Seminar V: Formations of the Unconscious* (R. Grigg, Trans.). Hoboken, NJ: Wiley.

Lacan, J. (1959–1960 [1992]). *Seminar VII: The Ethics of Psychoanalysis*. New York: W. W. Norton.

Lacan, J. (1960–1961 [2015]). *Seminar VIII: Transference* (B. Fink, Trans.). Cambridge: Polity.

Lacan, J. (1961–1962 [2002]). *Seminar IX: Identification* (C. Gallagher, Trans.). London: Karnac.

Lacan, J. (1962–1963 [2014]). *Seminar X: Anxiety* (J.-A. Miller, Ed.). Cambridge: Polity.

Lacan, J. (1966–1967). *La logique du fantasme*. Unpublished typescript.

Lacan, J. (1966 [2002]). *Écrits* (B. Fink, Trans.). New York: W. W. Norton.

Lacan, J. (1972–1973 [1998]). *Seminar XX: Encore—On Feminine Sexuality, the Limits of Love and Knowledge* (B. Fink, Trans.). London and New York: W. W. Norton.

Lacan, J. (1973 [1981]). *Four Fundamental Concepts of Psychoanalysis* (A. Sheridan, Trans.). New York: W. W. Norton.

Lacan, J. (1974–1975). *Seminar XXII: R.S.I.* (C. Gallagher, Trans.). Unofficial Edition.

Lacan, J. (1978–1979). *Seminar XXI: Les non-dupes errent* (C. Callagher, Trans.). Unofficial Edition.

La Rochefoucauld, F. (1959). *Maxims*. New York: Penguin Books.

McKerrow, R. B. (1966). *The Works of Thomas Nashe*. London: Blackwell.

Melville, H. (1853). *Bartleby the Scrivener: A Story of Wall Street*. New York: Putnam.

Milner, J.-C. (1995). *L'Œuvre claire, Lacan, la science, la philosophie*. Paris: Seuil.

Milner, J.-C. (2000). The Doctrine of Science. In O. Feltham (trans.), *Umbr(a): Science and Truth* (p. 1).

Nasio, J.-D. (1987). *Le silence en psychanalyse*. Paris: Payot.

Nobus, D. (2000). *Jacques Lacan and the Freudian Practice of Psychoanalysis*. London: Routledge.

Pascal, B. (1670 [2006]). *Pensées* (W. F. Trotter, Trans.). New York: Dutton and Company.

Peden, K., & Milner, J.-C. (2008). The Force of Minimalism: An Interview with Jean-Claude Milner. In P. Hallward & K. Peden (Eds.), *Concept and Form, Volume 2: Interviews and Essays on Cahiers pour l'analyse*. London and New York: Verso.

Reik, T. (1987 [1926]). Au début est le silence. In Sous la direction de J.-D. Nasio, *Le silence en psychanalyse* (pp. 18–46). Paris: Petite Bibliothèque Payot.

Roudinesco, E. (1994). *Histoire de la psychoanalyse en France II*. Paris: Fayard.

Roudinesco, E. (1997). *Jacques Lacan* (B. Bray, Trans.). New York: Columbia University Press.

Soler, C. (2006). *What Lacan Said About Women: A Psychoanalytic Study*. New York: Other Press.

Šumič-Riha, J. (2004). Testimony and the Real: Testimony Between the Impossibility and Obligation. *Parallax, 10*(1), 17–29.

Taylor, C. (2016). *The Language Animal: The Full Shape of the Human Linguistic Capacity*. Cambridge: Harvard University Press.

Valéry, P. (1917 [1997]). *La Jeune Parque* (A. Elliot, Trans.). Hexham: Bloodaxe Books.

Wittgenstein, L. (1922 [1981]). *Tractatus Logico-Philosophicus* (C. K. Ogden, Trans.). New York and London: Routledge.

Žižek, S. (1996). I Hear You with My Eyes. In S. Žižek & R. Salecl (Eds.), *Gaze and Voice as Love Objects*. Durham: Duke University Press.

Žižek, S. (2002). *Welcome to the Desert of the Real*. London: Verso.

Žižek, S. (2006). *The Parallax View*. Cambridge: MIT Press.

Zupančič, A. (2000). *The Ethics of the Real: Kant and Lacan*. London: Verso.

Index

E. Pluth and C. Zeiher, *On Silence*, The Palgrave Lacan Series, https://doi.org/10.1007/978-3-030-28147-2